OPPOSING VIEWPOINTS® SERIES

I0812911

Identity Politics

Other Books of Related Interest

Opposing Viewpoints Series

Diversity, Equity, and Inclusion
LGBTQIA+ Rights
The Politics of Gender and Sexuality

At Issue Series

Male Privilege
Mob Rule or the Wisdom of the Crowd?
Partisanship

Current Controversies Series

Libertarians, Socialists, and Other Third Parties
Nativism, Nationalism, and Patriotism
Reparations for Black Americans

> "Congress shall make no law . . . abridging the freedom of speech, or of the press."
>
> *First Amendment to the U.S. Constitution*

The basic foundation of our democracy is the First Amendment guarantee of freedom of expression. The Opposing Viewpoints series is dedicated to the concept of this basic freedom and the idea that it is more important to practice it than to enshrine it.

OPPOSING VIEWPOINTS® SERIES

Identity Politics

Martin Gitlin, Book Editor

GREENHAVEN PUBLISHING

Published in 2025 by Greenhaven Publishing, LLC
2544 Clinton Street,
Buffalo NY 14224

Copyright © 2025 by Greenhaven Publishing, LLC

First Edition

All rights reserved. No part of this book may be reproduced in any form without permission in writing from the publisher, except by a reviewer.

Articles in Greenhaven Publishing anthologies are often edited for length to meet page requirements. In addition, original titles of these works are changed to clearly present the main thesis and to explicitly indicate the author's opinion. Every effort is made to ensure that Greenhaven Publishing accurately reflects the original intent of the authors. Every effort has been made to trace the owners of the copyrighted material.

Cover image: Lightspring/Shutterstock.com

Library of Congress CataloginginPublication Data

Names: Gitlin, Marty, editor.
Title: Identity politics / edited by Martin Gitlin.
Description: First edition. | New York : Greenhaven Publishing,
2025. | Series: Opposing viewpoints | Includes index.
Identifiers: ISBN 9781534509955 (pbk.) | ISBN 9781534509962 (library bound)
Subjects: LCSH: Identity politics. | Group identity--Political
aspects. | Political culture -- United States.
Classification: LCC HM753.I346 2025 | DDC 306.2--dc23

Manufactured in the United States of America

Website: http://greenhavenpublishing.com

Contents

Chapter 3: Are Identity Politics Effective in Creating Political Change?

Chapter 4: How Much Do Identity Politics Contribute to Political and Social Polarization?

The Importance of Opposing Viewpoints

Perhaps every generation experiences a period in time in which the populace seems especially polarized, starkly divided on the important issues of the day and gravitating toward the far ends of the political spectrum and away from a consensus-facilitating middle ground. The world that today's students are growing up in and that they will soon enter into as active and engaged citizens is deeply fragmented in just this way. Issues relating to terrorism, immigration, women's rights, minority rights, race relations, health care, taxation, wealth and poverty, the environment, policing, military intervention, the proper role of government—in some ways, perennial issues that are freshly and uniquely urgent and vital with each new generation—are currently roiling the world.

If we are to foster a knowledgeable, responsible, active, and engaged citizenry among today's youth, we must provide them with the intellectual, interpretive, and critical-thinking tools and experience necessary to make sense of the world around them and of the all-important debates and arguments that inform it. After all, the outcome of these debates will in large measure determine the future course, prospects, and outcomes of the world and its peoples, particularly its youth. If they are to become successful members of society and productive and informed citizens, students need to learn how to evaluate the strengths and weaknesses of someone else's arguments, how to sift fact from opinion and fallacy, and how to test the relative merits and validity of their own opinions against the known facts and the best possible available information. The landmark series Opposing Viewpoints has been providing students with just such critical-thinking skills and exposure to the debates surrounding society's most urgent contemporary issues for many years, and it continues to serve this essential role with undiminished commitment, care, and rigor.

The key to the series's success in achieving its goal of sharpening students' critical-thinking and analytic skills resides in its title—

Opposing Viewpoints. In every intriguing, compelling, and engaging volume of this series, readers are presented with the widest possible spectrum of distinct viewpoints, expert opinions, and informed argumentation and commentary, supplied by some of today's leading academics, thinkers, analysts, politicians, policy makers, economists, activists, change agents, and advocates. Every opinion and argument anthologized here is presented objectively and accorded respect. There is no editorializing in any introductory text or in the arrangement and order of the pieces. No piece is included as a "straw man," an easy ideological target for cheap point-scoring. As wide and inclusive a range of viewpoints as possible is offered, with no privileging of one particular political ideology or cultural perspective over another. It is left to each individual reader to evaluate the relative merits of each argument—as they see it, and with the use of ever-growing critical-thinking skills—and grapple with their own assumptions, beliefs, and perspectives to determine how convincing or successful any given argument is and how the reader's own stance on the issue may be modified or altered in response to it.

This process is facilitated and supported by volume, chapter, and selection introductions that provide readers with the essential context they need to begin engaging with the spotlighted issues, with the debates surrounding them, and with their own perhaps shifting or nascent opinions on them. In addition, guided reading and discussion questions encourage readers to determine the authors' point of view and purpose, interrogate and analyze the various arguments and their rhetoric and structure, evaluate the arguments' strengths and weaknesses, test their claims against available facts and evidence, judge the validity of the reasoning, and bring into clearer, sharper focus the reader's own beliefs and conclusions and how they may differ from or align with those in the collection or those of their classmates.

Research has shown that reading comprehension skills improve dramatically when students are provided with compelling, intriguing, and relevant "discussable" texts. The subject matter of these collections could not be more compelling, intriguing, or urgently relevant to today's students and the world they are poised to inherit. The anthologized articles and the reading and discussion questions that are included with them also provide the basis for stimulating, lively, and passionate classroom debates. Students who are compelled to anticipate objections to their own argument and identify the flaws in those of an opponent read more carefully, think more critically, and steep themselves in relevant context, facts, and information more thoroughly. In short, using discussable text of the kind provided by every single volume in the Opposing Viewpoints series encourages close reading, facilitates reading comprehension, fosters research, strengthens critical thinking, and greatly enlivens and energizes classroom discussion and participation. The entire learning process is deepened, extended, and strengthened.

For all of these reasons, Opposing Viewpoints continues to be exactly the right resource at exactly the right time—when we most need to provide readers with the critical-thinking tools and skills that will not only serve them well in school but also in their careers and their daily lives as decision-making family members, community members, and citizens. This series encourages respectful engagement with and analysis of opposing viewpoints and fosters a resulting increase in the strength and rigor of one's own opinions and stances. As such, it helps make readers "future ready," and that readiness will pay rich dividends for the readers themselves, for the citizenry, for our society, and for the world at large.

Introduction

> *"An important ethical function of identity politics, in this context, is to highlight that obstacles to the self-development of individuals, and to the formation and exercise of their agency, emerge in complex cultural and psychic forms, as well as through more familiar kinds of socio-economic inequality."*
>
> *—Michael Kenny, British political science professor*

The iconic 1960s rock band Buffalo Springfield were not referring to identity politics when they famously sang, "There's battle lines being drawn. Nobody's right if everybody's wrong." But the words certainly fit modern debate. Identity politics have created a clear distinction between right-wing and left-wing political beliefs. And everyone feels strongly they are morally justified in their views.

Identity politics has been defined as a political, social activity or outlook to further the cause of a particular racial, ethnic, cultural, religious, gender, or sexual orientation group with the goal of remedying historical or ongoing prejudices and injustices heaped upon them by those in power or others throughout society.

That is a broad definition, but identity politics has squarely placed Americans (perhaps more than any other nationality) on opposite sides of the fence. It has caused resentment about "wokeness" that has splintered Democrats and coalesced Republicans. Controversial advisor to former President Donald Trump, Steve Bannon, offered to liberal-leaning magazine the *American Prospect*:

> The Democrats, the longer they talk about identity politics, I got 'em. I want them to talk about racism every day. If the left is focused on race and identity, and we go with economic nationalism we can crush the Democrats.[1]

The polarizing impact of identity politics has often obscured its political potential. It has caused heated debate that has divided the United States. Its focus on marginalized people has perpetuated disagreements about how they have been mistreated in the past and present and whether social and political changes are required. That includes most significantly arguments on historical and current victimizations based on race and those in the LGBTQ+ community, but also religion, gender, and nationality. *Opposing Viewpoints: Identity Politics* will explore those issues. It will ask and debate various questions involving identity politics.

Is the notion that identity politics is a modern phenomenon accurate? Though not identified as identity politics, do the arguments about slavery leading up to the Civil War not fall under that category?

How has media—and especially social media—impacted the arguments about identity politics? Is it responsible for creating and exacerbating the problem?

What has been the impact of identity politics? Has it helped marginalized people gain rights and recognition? Or has it sown irreparable divisions in American society?

What is the future of identity politics? Will it slip away into the dustbin of history? Will it grow into a more divisive philosophy that causes greater social and political friction? Or might it be more widely accepted as a philosophy that aids marginalized people and brings Americans closer together? These are all questions viewpoints in this volume address and authors attempt to answer.

In some ways, identity politics has split the political left and coalesced the right. Left-leaning comedians and political commentators such as Bill Maher have chastized "woke" culture in its embracing of identity politics as harmful to Democrats as it rallies Republicans together in a common cause. But Democrats have also used identity politics to gain support as they brand Trump and right-wing Republicans as insensitive to the plight of anyone aside from those most would consider the privileged in American society.

The debates gained intensity in the aftermath of the murder of Black American George Floyd by Minneapolis police during the COVID pandemic of 2020 and the rise of the Black Lives Matter movement. But other issues such as whether trans women should be able to compete against cisgender women on athletic fields and use bathrooms previously segregated by gender assigned at birth also resulted in contentious news stories that further polarized the nation.

Though some trace identity politics back centuries, others claim its seeds were planted in the 1980s and 1990s as a reaction to a perceived lack of progress instituting the promises of equal treatment for Black Americans made during the Civil Rights Movement decades earlier and the battle for equality under and law and representation for the LGBTQ+ population of that era. It caused backlash when some claimed that affirmative action is reverse discrimination. This created obstacles to equal treatment for multiple marginalized groups, but particularly Black Americans and women.

The debate began and it slowly expanded as the number of groups considered marginalized grew and resentment against movements to aid their causes from opposition boiled over. Despite the heated political atmosphere this has contributed to, it has also created a great deal of social change for these groups, increasing awareness of the ways they are placed at a disadvantage by society and stoking interest in finding ways to correct these inequalities.

Many feel the goal of identity politics is to help the marginalized and that is a positive thing. But some also believe the result has been a contentious and even angry dialogue that has further split society, causing divisions that are feared irreparable. This book examines various perspectives on the issue, allowing readers to decide for themselves.

Notes

1. Robert Kuttner, "Steve Bannon Gets His Wish," the American Prospect, July 8, 2020, https://prospect.org/blogs-and-newsletters/tap/steve-bannon-gets-his-wish/.

OPPOSING VIEWPOINTS® SERIES

CHAPTER 1

Are Identity Politics a Contemporary Political Phenomenon?

Chapter Preface

Perhaps it's a matter of perception or semantics. Some claim that identity politics began dividing Americans and altering U.S. history before the Civil War (1861–1865), particularly in regard to slavery. Others believe that it was not truly conceptualized until the 1980s or even beyond, as issues surrounding racial and LGBTQ+ rights became more fractious. Many trace it to the Civil Rights, feminist, and gay rights (now known as LGBTQ+ rights) movements of the 1950s to 1970s.

This chapter explores history to provide greater insight and context for current identity politics. Though the term "identity politics" was first introduced in 1973 and has only made it into public political discourse in recent years, especially after the murder of George Floyd sparked nationwide protests and the Black Lives Matter movement was launched, one might even trace it back to before the Revolutionary War as some folks in the colonies continued for years to side with King George and the British while others sought to overthrow that government.

Should that be considered identity politics? It depends on one's definition. Are identity politics only reserved for marginalized groups? If so, should abolitionists who fought for the end of slavery be considered the first advocates of identity politics in the United States? What about those who called for the end of mistreatment of Native Americans throughout the 19th century?

Perhaps, however, the distant history of identity politics does not matter in the modern era. Those who offer that identity politics is only a contemporary phenomenon will cite that the number of marginalized groups that have gained acknowledgement has certainly grown in recent years. For instance, one might debate that the LGBTQ+ community was not considered marginalized before the 1970s because they had not previously formed an organized political movement and identity. Women gained recognition as a marginalized group particularly during the women's liberation movement of the 1960s to 1980s, which helped lead to the ratification of the Equal Rights Amendment in 1972, offering women equal rights in employment, property, legal matters, and pay.

Perhaps the debate about whether identity politics was born and thriving in centuries or at least decades past is irrelevant. Maybe all that matters is today. But it has been famously stated that those who do not learn from history are doomed to repeat it. And if that is indeed true, defining identity politics in historical terms becomes important in dealing with current discourse around identity and marginalization.

Viewpoint 1

> *"The American Revolution divided the colonists as much as it united them, with Loyalists (or Tories) joining the British forces against the Patriots (or revolutionaries)."*

Identity and Politics During the American Revolution

P. Scott Corbett, Volker Janssen, John M. Lund, Todd Pfannestiel, Sylvie Waskiewicz, and Paul Vickery

In this viewpoint, the authors discuss how identity based on politics as well as other characteristics became more of an issue during the American Revolutionary War (1775–1783). It explains how American colonists aligned themselves with the Loyalists (who supported Great Britain) and the Revolutionaries (who wanted independence from the British) and how this caused significant division. It also discusses the roles of enslaved Black people, Indigenous people, and women during the Revolution, and how that event offered them opportunities for greater empowerment depending on which group they aligned themselves with. P. Scott Corbett is a professor of history at Ventura College in California. Volker Janssen is a professor of history at California State University, Fullerton. John M. Lund is an adjunct professor of history at Franklin Pierce University in New Hampshire. Todd Pfannestiel is president of Utica University in New York. Sylvie

"Identity During the American Revolution" by P. Scott Corbett, Volker Janssen, John M. Lund, Todd Pfannestiel, Sylvie Waskiewicz, and Paul Vickery, OpenStaxCollege, December 30, 2014, https://openstax.org/books/us-history/pages/6-4-identity-during-the-american-revolution. Licensed under CC BY 4.0 International.

Waskiewicz is an editor with a PhD in French Studies from New York University. Paul Vickery was a professor of history at Oral Roberts University in Oklahoma.

As you read, consider the following questions:

1. Approximately what percentage of British Americans remained loyal to Great Britain?
2. What are confiscation acts?
3. According to this viewpoint, which side was it more advantageous for enslaved Black people and Indigenous people to align with? Why was this the case?

The American Revolution in effect created multiple civil wars. Many of the resentments and antagonisms that fed these conflicts predated the Revolution, and the outbreak of war acted as the catalyst they needed to burst forth. In particular, the middle colonies of New York, New Jersey, and Pennsylvania had deeply divided populations. Loyalty to Great Britain came in many forms, from wealthy elites who enjoyed the prewar status quo to runaway slaves who desired the freedom that the British offered.

Loyalists

Historians disagree on what percentage of colonists were Loyalists; estimates range from 20 percent to over 30 percent. In general, however, of British America's population of 2.5 million, roughly one-third remained loyal to Great Britain, while another third committed themselves to the cause of independence. The remaining third remained apathetic, content to continue with their daily lives as best they could and preferring not to engage in the struggle.

Many Loyalists were royal officials and merchants with extensive business ties to Great Britain, who viewed themselves as the rightful and just defenders of the British Constitution. Others simply resented local business and political rivals who supported the Revolution, viewing the rebels as hypocrites and schemers who selfishly used the break with the empire to increase their fortunes. In New York's Hudson Valley, animosity among the tenants of estates owned by revolutionary leaders turned them to the cause of king and empire.

During the war, all the states passed confiscation acts, which gave the new revolutionary governments in the former colonies the right to seize Loyalist land and property. To ferret out Loyalists, revolutionary governments also passed laws requiring the male population to take oaths of allegiance to the new states. Those who refused lost their property and were often imprisoned or made to work for the new local revolutionary order.

William Franklin, Benjamin Franklin's only surviving son, remained loyal to crown and empire and served as royal governor of New Jersey, a post he secured with his father's help. During the war, revolutionaries imprisoned William in Connecticut; however, he remained steadfast in his allegiance to Great Britain and moved to England after the Revolution. He and his father never reconciled.

As many as nineteen thousand colonists served the British in the effort to put down the rebellion, and after the Revolution, as many as 100,000 colonists left, moving to England or north to Canada rather than staying in the new United States. Eight thousand whites and five thousand free Blacks went to Britain. Over thirty thousand went to Canada, transforming that nation from predominately French to predominantly British. Another sizable group of Loyalists went to the British West Indies, taking their slaves with them.

Slaves and Indians

While some slaves who fought for the patriot cause received their freedom, revolutionary leaders—unlike the British—did not grant such slaves their freedom as a matter of course. Washington, the owner of more than two hundred slaves during the Revolution, refused to let slaves serve in the army, although he did allow free Blacks. (In his will, Washington did free his slaves.) In the new United States, the Revolution largely reinforced a racial identity based on skin color. Whiteness, now a national identity, denoted freedom and stood as the key to power. Blackness, more than ever before, denoted servile status. Indeed, despite their class and ethnic differences, white revolutionaries stood mostly united in their hostility to both Blacks and Indians.

For slaves willing to run away and join the British, the American Revolution offered a unique occasion to escape bondage. Of the half a million slaves in the American colonies during the Revolution, twenty thousand joined the British cause. At Yorktown, for instance, thousands of Black troops fought with Lord Cornwallis. Slaves belonging to George Washington, Thomas Jefferson, Patrick Henry, and other revolutionaries seized the opportunity for freedom and fled to the British side. Between ten and twenty thousand slaves gained their freedom because of the Revolution; arguably, the Revolution created the largest slave uprising and the greatest emancipation until the Civil War. After the Revolution, some of these African Loyalists emigrated to Sierra Leone on the west coast of Africa. Others removed to Canada and England. It is also true that people of color made heroic contributions to the cause of American independence. However, while the British offered slaves freedom, most American revolutionaries clung to notions of Black inferiority.

Powerful Indian peoples who had allied themselves with the British, including the Mohawk and the Creek, also remained loyal to the Empire. A Mohawk named Joseph Brant, whose given name was Thayendanegea, rose to prominence while fighting for the British during the Revolution. He joined forces with Colonel Barry St. Leger during the 1777 campaign, which ended with the surrender of General Burgoyne at Saratoga. After the war, Brant moved to the Six Nations reserve in Canada. From his home on the shores of Lake Ontario, he remained active in efforts to restrict white encroachment onto Indian lands. After their defeat, the British did not keep promises they'd made to help their Indian allies keep their territory; in fact, the Treaty of Paris granted the United States huge amounts of supposedly British-owned regions that were actually Indian lands.

Patriots

The American revolutionaries (also called patriots or Whigs) came from many different backgrounds and included merchants, shoemakers, farmers, and sailors. What is extraordinary is the way in which the struggle for independence brought a vast cross-section of society together, animated by a common cause.

During the war, the revolutionaries faced great difficulties, including massive supply problems; clothing, ammunition, tents, and equipment were all hard to come by. After an initial burst of enthusiasm in 1775 and 1776, the shortage of supplies became acute in 1777 through 1779, as Washington's difficult winter at Valley Forge demonstrates.

Funding the war effort also proved very difficult. Whereas the British could pay in gold and silver, the American forces relied on paper money, backed by loans obtained in Europe. This first American money was called Continental currency; unfortunately, it quickly fell in value. "Not worth a Continental" soon became a shorthand term for something of no value. The new revolutionary government printed a great amount of this paper money, resulting in runaway inflation. By 1781, inflation was such that 146 Continental dollars were worth only one dollar in gold. The problem grew worse as each former colony, now a revolutionary state, printed its own currency.

Women

In colonial America, women shouldered enormous domestic and child-rearing responsibilities. The war for independence only increased their workload and, in some ways, solidified their roles. Rebel leaders required women to produce articles for war—everything from clothing to foodstuffs—while also keeping their homesteads going. This was not an easy task when their husbands and sons were away fighting. Women were also expected to provide food and lodging for armies and to nurse wounded soldiers.

The Revolution opened some new doors for women, however, as they took on public roles usually reserved for men. The Daughters of Liberty, an informal organization formed in the mid-1760s to oppose British revenue-raising measures, worked tirelessly to support the war effort. Esther DeBerdt Reed of Philadelphia, wife of Governor Joseph Reed, formed the Ladies Association of Philadelphia and led a fundraising drive to provide sorely needed supplies to the Continental Army. In "The Sentiments of an American Woman" (1780), she wrote to other women, "The time is arrived to display the same sentiments which animated us at the beginning of the Revolution, when we renounced the use of teas, however agreeable to our taste, rather than receive them from our persecutors; when we made it appear to them that we placed former necessaries in the rank of superfluities, when our liberty was interested; when our republican and laborious hands spun the flax, prepared the linen intended for the use of our soldiers; when exiles and fugitives we supported with courage all the evils which are the concomitants of war." Reed and other elite women in Philadelphia raised almost $300,000 in Continental money for the war.

Women who did not share Reed's elite status nevertheless played key economic roles by producing homespun cloth and food. During shortages, some women formed mobs and wrested supplies from those who hoarded them. Crowds of women beset merchants and demanded fair prices for goods; if a merchant refused, a riot would ensue. Still other women accompanied the army as "camp followers," serving as cooks, washerwomen, and nurses. A few also took part in combat and proved their equality with men through violence against the hated British.

Section Summary

The American Revolution divided the colonists as much as it united them, with Loyalists (or Tories) joining the British forces against the patriots (or revolutionaries). Both sides included a broad cross-section of the population. However, Great Britain was able to convince many slaves to join its forces by promising them freedom, something the southern revolutionaries would not agree to do. The war provided new opportunities, as well as new challenges, for slaves, free Blacks, women, and Indians. After the war, many Loyalists fled the American colonies, heading across the Atlantic to England, north to Canada, or south to the West Indies.

Viewpoint 2

> *"In the late 1960s and early 1970s, many young people came to embrace a new wave of cultural dissent."*

Identity Politics Develop in a Fractured American Society

P. Scott Corbett, Volker Janssen, John M. Lund, Todd Pfannestiel, Sylvie Waskiewicz, and Paul Vickery

In this viewpoint, the authors explain how the late 1960s and 1970s were an era of great political change in the United States, especially for marginalized groups, and how the rise of identity politics facilitated these changes. The counterculture of this era promoted dissent for the status quo, characterizing a time when people began to question the social order. At the same time, American Indians, LGBTQ+ people, and women began to protest for their rights. While this wide range of protests created a great deal of tension in the United States, it also led to positive social change for many of these groups. P. Scott Corbett is a professor of history at Ventura College in California. Volker Janssen is a professor of history at California State University, Fullerton. John M. Lund is an adjunct professor of history at Franklin Pierce University in New Hampshire. Todd Pfannestiel is president of Utica University in New York. Sylvie Waskiewicz is an editor with a PhD in French Studies from New York University. Paul Vickery was a professor of history at Oral Roberts University in Oklahoma.

"Identity Politics in a Fractured Society" by P. Scott Corbett, Volker Janssen, John M. Lund, Todd Pfannestiel, Sylvie Waskiewicz, and Paul Vickery, OpenStaxCollege, December 30, 2014, https://openstax.org/books/us-history/pages/30-1-identity-politics-in-a-fractured-society. Licensed under CC BY 4.0 International.

As you read, consider the following questions:

1. What was the Stonewall Inn? Why was it significant to the gay rights movement?
2. What do the authors credit for the advancement in women's rights during the 1960s and 1970s?
3. Why did men in the Congressional Black Caucus disagree with Shirley Chisholm?

The political divisions that plagued the United States in the 1960s were reflected in the rise of identity politics in the 1970s. As people lost hope of reuniting as a society with common interests and goals, many focused on issues of significance to the subgroups to which they belonged, based on culture, ethnicity, sexual orientation, gender, and religion.

Hippies and the Counterculture

In the late 1960s and early 1970s, many young people came to embrace a new wave of cultural dissent. The counterculture offered an alternative to the bland homogeneity of American middle-class life, patriarchal family structures, self-discipline, unquestioning patriotism, and the acquisition of property. In fact, there were many alternative cultures.

"Hippies" rejected the conventions of traditional society. Men sported beards and grew their hair long; both men and women wore clothing from non-Western cultures, defied their parents, rejected social etiquettes and manners, and turned to music as an expression of their sense of self. Casual sex between unmarried men and women was acceptable. Drug use, especially of marijuana and psychedelic drugs like LSD and peyote, was common. Most hippies were also deeply attracted to the ideas of peace and freedom. They protested the war in Vietnam and preached a doctrine of personal freedom to be and act as one wished.

Some hippies dropped out of mainstream society altogether and expressed their disillusionment with the cultural and spiritual limitations of American freedom. They joined communes, usually in rural areas, to share a desire to live closer to nature, respect for the earth, a dislike of modern life, and a disdain for wealth and material goods. Many communes grew their own organic food. Others abolished the concept of private property, and all members shared willingly with one another. Some sought to abolish traditional ideas regarding love and marriage, and free love was practiced openly. One of the most famous communes was The Farm, established in Tennessee in 1971. Residents adopted a blend of Christian and Asian beliefs. They shared housing, owned no private property except tools and clothing, advocated nonviolence, and tried to live as one with nature, becoming vegetarians and avoiding the use of animal products. They smoked marijuana in an effort to reach a higher state of consciousness and to achieve a feeling of oneness and harmony.

Music, especially rock and folk music, occupied an important place in the counterculture. Concerts provided the opportunity to form seemingly impromptu communities to celebrate youth, rebellion, and individuality. In mid-August 1969, nearly 400,000 people attended a music festival in rural Bethel, New York, many for free. They jammed roads throughout the state, and thousands had to be turned around and sent home. Thirty-two acts performed for a crowd that partook freely of marijuana, LSD, and alcohol during the rainy three-day event that became known as Woodstock (after the nearby town) and became the cultural touchstone of a generation. No other event better symbolized the cultural independence and freedom of Americans coming of age in the 1960s.

American Indian Protest

As the young, primarily White men and women who became hippies strove to create new identities for themselves, they borrowed liberally from other cultures, including that of Native

Americans. At the same time, many Native Americans were themselves seeking to maintain their culture or retrieve elements that had been lost. In 1968, a group of American Indian activists, including Dennis Banks, George Mitchell, and Clyde Bellecourt, convened a gathering of two hundred people in Minneapolis, Minnesota, and formed the American Indian Movement (AIM). The organizers were urban dwellers frustrated by decades of poverty and discrimination. In 1970, the average life expectancy of Native Americans was forty-six years compared to the national average of sixty-nine. The suicide rate was twice that of the general population, and the infant mortality rate was the highest in the country. Half of all Native Americans lived on reservations, where unemployment reached 50 percent. Among those in cities, 20 percent lived below the poverty line.

On November 20, 1969, a small group of Native American activists landed on Alcatraz Island (the former site of a notorious federal prison) in San Francisco Bay. They announced plans to build an American Indian cultural center, including a history museum, an ecology center, and a spiritual sanctuary. People on the mainland provided supplies by boat, and celebrities visited Alcatraz to publicize the cause. More people joined the occupiers until, at one point, they numbered about four hundred. From the beginning, the federal government negotiated with them to persuade them to leave. They were reluctant to accede, but over time, the occupiers began to drift away of their own accord. Government forces removed the final holdouts on June 11, 1971, nineteen months after the occupation began.

The next major demonstration came in 1972 when AIM members and others marched on Washington, D.C.—a journey they called the "Trail of Broken Treaties"—and occupied the offices of the Bureau of Indian Affairs (BIA). The group presented a list of demands, which included improved housing, education, and economic opportunities in Native American communities; the drafting of new treaties; the return of Native lands; and protections for Native religions and culture.

The most dramatic event staged by AIM was the occupation of the community of Wounded Knee, South Dakota, in February 1973. Wounded Knee, on the Pine Ridge Indian Reservation, had historical significance: It was the site of an 1890 massacre of members of the Lakota tribe by the U.S. Army. AIM went to the reservation following the failure of a group of Oglala to impeach the tribal president Dick Wilson, whom they accused of corruption and the use of strong-arm tactics to silence critics. AIM used the occasion to criticize the U.S. government for failing to live up to its treaties with native peoples.

The federal government surrounded the area with U.S. marshals, FBI agents, and other law enforcement forces. A siege ensued that lasted seventy-one days, with frequent gunfire from both sides, wounding a U.S. marshal as well as an FBI agent, and killing two Native Americans. The government did very little to meet the protesters' demands. Two AIM leaders, Dennis Banks and Russell Means, were arrested, but charges were later dismissed. The Nixon administration had already halted the federal policy of termination and restored millions of acres to tribes. Increased funding for Native American education, healthcare, legal services, housing, and economic development followed, along with the hiring of more Native American employees in the BIA.

Gay Rights

Combined with the sexual revolution and the feminist movement of the 1960s, the counterculture helped establish a climate that fostered the struggle for gay and lesbian rights. Lesbian, gay, bisexual, transgender, and queer people (later abbreviated as LGBTQ) had long been denied rights and had been perceived as threatening. As discussed earlier, LGBTQ veterans were dishonorably discharged without benefits, and LGBTQ people were cast under a cloud of suspicion during the McCarthy era. But that mistreatment was only a small part of the anti-gay oppression. By most considerations, LGBTQ people's very existence was criminalized. Sexual relations between same-sex couples were illegal in most states until the 1980s, and various city and state ordinances disallowed members of the same sex from dancing or even holding hands with each other. Other laws were used to require that people wear clothing deemed appropriate to their gender. These statutes gave authorities the ability to harass, detain, arrest, sexually humiliate, and prosecute people for their identity. Perhaps worse, it led to extensive anti-LGBTQ violence that was rarely investigated or prosecuted.

Many gay rights groups were founded in Los Angeles and San Francisco, cities that were administrative centers in the network of U.S. military installations and the places where many gay men suffered dishonorable discharges. The first postwar organization for gay and lesbian civil rights, the Mattachine Society, was launched in Los Angeles in 1950. The first national organization for lesbians, the Daughters of Bilitis, was founded in San Francisco five years later. In 1966, the city became home to the world's first organization for transgender people, the National Transsexual Counseling Unit (transsexual was a more commonly used term at the time); and in 1967, the Sexual Freedom League of San Francisco was born.

Through these organizations and others, LGBTQ activists fought against the criminalization and discrimination of their sexual identities on a number of occasions throughout the 1960s, employing strategies of both protests and litigation. However, the most famous event in the gay rights movement took place not in San Francisco but in New York City. Early in the morning of June 28, 1969, police raided a Greenwich Village gay bar called the Stonewall Inn. Although such raids were common, the response of the Stonewall patrons was anything but. As the police prepared to arrest many of the customers, especially transgender people, who were particular targets for police harassment, a crowd began to gather. Angered by the brutal treatment of the prisoners, the crowd attacked. Beer bottles and bricks were thrown. The police barricaded themselves inside the bar and waited for reinforcements. The riot continued for several hours and resumed the following night. Shortly thereafter, activists formed the Gay Liberation Front and Gay Activists' Alliance and began to protest discrimination, homophobia, and violence against gay people, promoting gay liberation and gay pride.

With a call for gay men and women to "come out"—a consciousness-raising campaign that shared many principles with the counterculture, gay and lesbian communities moved from the urban underground into the political sphere. Gay rights activists protested strongly against the official position of the American Psychiatric Association (APA), which categorized homosexuality as a mental illness and often resulted in job loss, loss of custody, and other serious personal consequences. By 1974, the APA had ceased to classify homosexuality as a form of mental illness but continued to consider it a "sexual orientation disturbance." Nevertheless, in 1974, Kathy Kozachenko became the first openly lesbian woman voted into office in Ann Arbor, Michigan. In 1977, Harvey Milk became California's first openly gay man elected to public office, although his service on San Francisco's board of supervisors, along with that of San Francisco mayor George Moscone, was cut short by the bullet of disgruntled former city supervisor Dan White.

One of the first steps toward greater LGTBQ rights was the decriminalization of relations. While police harassment would continue and hate crimes would escalate, the elimination of criminality simply for being gay was an important and consequential initial victory. Illinois was the first state to decriminalize same-sex relations in 1962, but was joined by only one other state (Connecticut) in the 1960s. The next decade saw 18 more states eliminate the bans, and the rest of the nation gradually reduced penalties or ceased enforcement of their codes. But in many cases, since nearly half of the states had such laws on the books, they could be used to justify a range of discriminatory acts and practices. (Consensual same-sex relations would be made legal nationwide in 2003 due to a Supreme Court decision.)

Maybe Not Now

The feminist push for greater rights continued through the 1970s. The media often ridiculed feminists as "women's libbers" and focused on more radical organizations like W.I.T.C.H. (Women's International Terrorist Conspiracy from Hell), a loose association of activist groups. Many reporters stressed the most unusual goals of the most radical women—calls for the abolition of marriage and demands that manholes be renamed "personholes."

The majority of feminists, however, sought meaningful accomplishments. In the 1970s, they opened battered women's shelters and successfully fought for protection from employment discrimination for pregnant women, reform of rape laws (such as the abolition of laws requiring a witness to corroborate a woman's report of rape), criminalization of domestic violence, and funding for schools that sought to counter sexist stereotypes of women. In 1973, the U.S. Supreme Court in *Roe v. Wade* invalidated a number of state laws under which abortions obtained during the first three months of pregnancy were illegal. This made a nontherapeutic abortion a legal medical procedure nationwide.

Many advances in women's rights were the result of women's greater engagement in politics. For example, Patsy Mink, the first Asian American woman elected to Congress, was the co-author of the Education Amendments Act of 1972, Title IX of which prohibits sex discrimination in education. Mink had been interested in fighting discrimination in education since her youth, when she opposed racial segregation in campus housing while a student at the University of Nebraska. She went to law school after being denied admission to medical school because of her gender. Like Mink, many other women sought and won political office, many with the help of the National Women's Political Caucus (NWPC). In 1971, the NWPC was formed by Bella Abzug, Gloria Steinem, Shirley Chisholm, Myrlie Evers-Williams, and other leading feminists to encourage women's participation in political parties, elect women to office, and raise money for their campaigns.

Shirley Chisholm personally took up the mantle of women's involvement in politics. Born of immigrant parents, she earned degrees from Brooklyn College and Columbia University, and began a career in early childhood education and advocacy. In the 1950's she joined various political action groups, worked on election campaigns, and pushed for housing and economic reforms. After leaving one organization over its refusal to involve women in the decision-making process, she sought to increase gender and racial diversity within political and activist organizations throughout New York City. In 1968, she became the first Black woman elected to Congress. Refusing to take the quiet role expected of new representatives, she immediately began sponsoring bills and initiatives. She spoke out against the Vietnam War, and fought for programs such as Head Start and the national school lunch program, which was eventually signed into law after Chisholm led an effort to override a presidential veto. Chisholm would eventually undertake a groundbreaking presidential run in 1972.

As a presidential candidate, Chisholm faced pressure from an unexpected source: her closest colleagues. Men within the Congressional Black Caucus, which she co-founded, disagreed with her pluralistic political coalition. The Democratic party did not allow her to participate in the televised primary debates, and she was only allowed one speech. She noted, "Black male politicians are no different from white male politicians. This 'woman thing' is so deep. I've found it out in this campaign if I never knew it before." Despite all this, Shirley Chisholm earned ten percent of the total Democratic delegates, and became a nationally influential figure.

The ultimate political goal of the National Organization for Women (NOW) was the passage of an Equal Rights Amendment (ERA). The amendment passed Congress in March 1972, and was sent to the states for ratification with a deadline of seven years for passage; if the amendment was not ratified by thirty-eight states by 1979, it would die. Twenty-two states ratified the ERA in 1972, and eight more in 1973. In the next two years, only four states voted for the amendment. In 1979, still four votes short, the amendment received a brief reprieve when Congress agreed to a three-year extension, but it never passed, as the result of the well-organized opposition of Christian and other socially conservative, grassroots organizations.

Viewpoint 3

> *"Identity politics is often criticized for reducing individuals to a single aspect of their identity, such as race, gender, or sexual orientation. This can ignore the complexity and multidimensionality of human experiences."*

How History Shaped Identity Politics

Steven Mintz

In this viewpoint, Steven Mintz argues that the history of identity politics extends decades beyond what is often cited as its launch in the late 20th century. He traces it back to the Civil Rights Movement of the 1950s and 1960s into the Black Power movement that followed. He claims those battles set the framework for what was to come and acknowledges that history shows identity politics can be a double-edged sword, offering the opportunity for political and social change as well as division. Steven Mintz is an American historian at the University of Texas at Austin.

As you read, consider the following questions:

1. What factors does Mintz credit for the rise in identity politics?
2. How did this viewpoint relate centuries-old philosophers to identity politics?

"Identity Politics: A Doubled-Edged Sword" by Steven Mintz, Professor of History, The University of Texas at Austin. Inside Higher Ed. Reprinted by Permission.

3. What criticism of identity politics does Mintz point out in this viewpoint?

Tell me a person's ethnic identity and I'll tell you their stance on the war in Gaza.

If nothing else, the conflict in the Middle East has made it clear that identity politics isn't going away. In fact, many individuals who previously criticized identity politics now embrace their personal identities more strongly than ever.

Identity politics refers to political positions and perspectives that focus on the interests and issues pertinent to specific groups defined by characteristics such as race, gender, sexuality, religion, nationality or other markers of identity. It emphasizes the distinct experiences and challenges faced by these groups and advocates for policies and practices that address their specific needs and rights.

Identity politics emerged prominently in the 1960s and 1970s during a period of significant social and political upheaval. Among the factors that contributed to its rise include:

- The Civil Rights Movements: The struggle for racial equality in the United States highlighted the distinct and systemic issues faced by African Americans, leading to a greater focus on race as a central axis of political struggle. The Black freedom struggle was accompanied by many other struggles for equality, including those waged by Chicanos and Native Americans. These movements exposed systemic inequalities and demanded recognition and rights for marginalized groups.
- The Black Power Movement: This movement stressed the importance of Black identity, self-determination and racial pride in the face of systemic and structural racism. This movement further solidified the role of identity in political activism.
- The Women's Liberation Movement: The feminist movement brought attention to gender-based inequalities and the unique

experiences of women, advocating for gender-specific rights and reforms.

- The LGBTQ+ Rights Movement: The fight for LGBTQ+ rights underscored the need for recognition and protection of sexual orientation and gender identity.
- Decolonization: The movement to end European colonialism emphasized the rights of indigenous and colonized peoples to sovereignty and self-determination.
- Transnationalism: Migration, diasporas and the movement of people, ideas, information and things across national borders have become important topics of study, requiring an understanding of how identities are formed and negotiated across borders.

The theoretical foundations of identity politics can be traced to works in critical theory, postcolonial studies, feminist theory and intersectionality.

The Frankfurt School, particularly thinkers like Herbert Marcuse and Theodor Adorno, emphasized the ways in which cultural and social structures maintain power and oppression. Their work laid the groundwork for understanding how identity and social position can shape one's experience of power and resistance.

In works like *Black Skin, White Masks* and *The Wretched of the Earth*, Frantz Fanon explored the psychological and cultural dimensions of colonialism and the struggle for liberation. His analysis of the dehumanizing effects of colonialism on both colonizers and the colonized provided a critical framework for understanding the intersections of race, identity and power.

Edward Said's *Orientalism* critiqued the ways that Western societies construct and perpetuate stereotypes about the East, illustrating how knowledge production is intertwined with power and identity. His work stressed the role of cultural representation in maintaining colonial dominance.

Simone de Beauvoir in *The Second Sex* analyzed the construction of women as "Other" and explored how gender identity is shaped by social and cultural forces. Her work is foundational for understanding gender as a critical aspect of identity. Later works, beginning with Betty Friedan's *The Feminine Mystique*, emphasized the need to recognize and address gender-based oppression.

Postmodernist thinkers like Michel Foucault and Jacques Derrida deconstructed grand narratives and challenged the idea of universal experiences. Instead, they focused on how power and knowledge are intertwined with identity.

The concept of intersectionality, introduced by Kimberlé Crenshaw, a leading scholar of critical race theory and Black feminist legal thought, called attention to the ways that various aspects of identity (such as race, gender, class and sexuality) intersect to produce distinctive experiences of oppression and privilege. This theoretical framework has become a cornerstone in understanding the complexities of identity.

Stuart Hall's work in cultural studies emphasized the role of media and culture in shaping identities and perpetuating power structures. He explored how cultural representation and identity politics intersect, particularly in the context of race, class and ethnicity.

Meanwhile, Queer Theory, especially Judith Butler's *Gender Trouble* and Eve Kosofsky Sedgwick's *Epistemology of the Closet*, challenged the binary understanding of gender and introduced the idea of gender performativity. Their works also questioned the stability of gender identities and emphasized the fluid and constructed nature of sexual and gender identities and laid bare the societal norms that shape and constrain sexual expression.

The historian and cultural critic Jackson Lears has described identity politics as a tragic necessity. His words capture the dual-edged nature of the societal, political and cultural impact of identity politics. On the one hand, identity politics is necessary for recognizing and addressing the specific needs and injustices faced by marginalized groups, promoting visibility, representation and empowerment.

On the other hand, identity politics can foster division, identity essentialism, a sense of victimhood and political co-optation. The

The National Woman's Party

On June 20, 1917, National Woman's Party (NWP) co-founder Lucy Burns took up her position on the sidewalk in front of the White House entry gate. Burns and NWP member Dora Lewis held between them a large banner addressed "To the Envoys of Russia." The banner accused President Woodrow Wilson of deceiving the Russians when he claimed that the two countries were fighting to preserve democracy. "We, the Women of America, tell you that America is not a democracy," the banner read. "Twenty million American Women are denied the right to vote. President Wilson is the chief opponent of their national enfranchisement." The Russian delegation saw the banner as their car passed through the White House gate on their way to meet with the president.

The National Woman's Party had organized pickets of the White House for six days a week, in all kinds of weather, since January 10, 1917. The "Silent Sentinels" as they were known showed up each day holding banners demanding the right to vote for American women. Rather than pursue enfranchisement state by state, as the National American Women's Suffrage Association (NAWSA) was doing, the NWP focused their efforts on the passage of an amendment to the U.S. Constitution. The amendment, named for Susan B. Anthony and first introduced in 1878, stated that "The right of citizens of the United States to vote shall not be denied or abridged by the United States or by any State on account of sex."

The NWP strategy to promote passage of the Anthony Amendment included pressuring President Wilson to support it. Presidents have no role in amending the Constitution, but NWP leader Alice Paul believed that Wilson's endorsement would sway members of Congress from the Democratic Party to vote for the amendment's passage. Their efforts had only managed to push Wilson to offer tepid support for women's suffrage eventually, although he asked for patience, chiding American women that "you can afford a little while to wait."

"National Woman's Party Protests During World War I," National Parks Service.

challenge lies in balancing the need for identity-based advocacy with the pursuit of broader social cohesion and universal principles of justice.

Identity politics, while a powerful tool for highlighting and addressing the specific needs and experiences of marginalized groups, also faces significant criticisms.

Critics argue that identity politics contributes to social fragmentation by emphasizing differences rather than commonalities, creating divisions within society, as different groups focus on their own specific interests rather than broader collective goals.

A stress on group identities can exacerbate tensions and provoke backlash from those who feel excluded or threatened by these movements, further entrenching divisions and making it challenging to build coalitions or find common ground.

Identity politics is often criticized for reducing individuals to a single aspect of their identity, such as race, gender, or sexual orientation. This can ignore the complexity and multidimensionality of human experiences. There is also a risk of reinforcing stereotypes and essentialist notions of identity, where individuals are seen primarily through the lens of their group affiliation rather than as unique individuals.

Certainly, identity politics can sometimes lead to the exclusion of voices within the same group that do not conform to the dominant narrative or ideology. This can create a form of gatekeeping where only certain perspectives are deemed legitimate.

There is also a concern that identity politics can foster a victimhood mentality. This can potentially undermine agency and resilience, focusing more on grievances than on empowerment and solutions.

Other sources of concern include tokenism and elite co-optation. The focus on identity can sometimes lead to tokenistic gestures rather than substantive changes, where symbolic representation is prioritized over meaningful policy or structural reforms. It's also the case that political elites and organizations use identity issues to advance their own agendas without genuinely addressing the underlying problems faced by marginalized groups.

Why, then, is identity politics so powerful? Because it provides a framework for marginalized groups to articulate their specific experiences of oppression, seeking recognition and redress. It also fosters a sense of solidarity and collective identity among members of marginalized groups, empowering them to advocate for their rights and interests.

Identity politics is a powerful tool for political mobilization, bringing together individuals who share common experiences and goals to advocate for equity, inclusion and policy changes. Identity politics has been instrumental in increasing the visibility and representation of marginalized groups in political, social and cultural spheres.

Can—should—anything be done to mute the emphasis on identity politics? If so, how?

One potential strategy is to stress universalism, addressing the needs of all citizens regardless of identity, focusing on shared human rights and common interests. We could foster inclusive narratives that highlight commonalities among different groups while respecting their unique experiences.

Emphasizing intersectionality to show how various identities overlap and interconnect can also help downplay broad identities, by underscoring identities' complexities. And, of course, promoting dialogue across different identity groups can build bridges and reduce divisiveness.

But there are costs to downplaying identity politics. De-emphasizing identity politics might result in overlooking the specific needs and experiences of marginalized groups, and further disempowering marginalized communities by muting their voice.

Ignoring identity-based issues could contribute to the erasure of historical injustices and the ongoing impact of systemic oppression. Reducing the emphasis on identity politics might also result in decreased visibility and representation of diverse groups in political and social arenas.

The challenge lies in finding ways to address the unique concerns of different groups while promoting unity and common ground.

I'm of the view that every contemporary issue—the pandemic, the reckoning with race, the Middle East conflict, and yes, identity politics—should be treated as a learning opportunity.

So, What Could Colleges Do?

They might offer a foundational course to provide an overview of identity politics, its historical development, key concepts and underlying theories, as well as its political impact.

Such a course should include an introduction to identity construction, examining how people's identities are constructed, socialized and internalized through family, education and other social institutions, as well as media representations of various identities and their impact on public perception and policy.

Particular attention should be paid to the psychological processes that underlie identity formation, the question of how social norms and roles are internalized, and the impact of identity on mental health and well-being.

This class should also explore the role of identity in political mobilization, policymaking and ideological debates, and compare and contrast identity politics in different countries and political systems. I hope that such a course would include experiential, outreach and cultural components, which might include field research, intercultural dialogue and participation in cross-cultural events.

A foundational course on identity politics can be a valuable learning experience for today's students. After all, in recent decades the study of identity has become central to the social sciences. Historians, political scientists, psychologists and sociologists have explored how identities are constructed, defined, cultivated and internalized; how identities shape perceptions, behavior and individuals' sense of self; and how social institutions, power structures, cultural norms and media representations influence and reinforce cognitive frameworks, role expectations, and political behavior and attitudes.

First of all, such a course can contribute to an understanding of the multidimensional nature of identity and how various aspects of identity intersect and shape experiences of privilege and oppression. It can also demonstrate that identity isn't a single, static attribute, but is a construction and its nature and salience has changed over time.

Secondly, such a course can integrate diverse disciplinary perspectives and methodologies. For example, sociology provides an understanding of how identities are constructed and maintained within societal structures and institutions, while psychology explores how identities are internalized and influence individual behavior and mental health. Meanwhile, political science examines the role of identity in political mobilization, policymaking and ideological debates, while history offers insights into the evolution of identity politics and the impact of historical events and movements.

Third, learning about the experiences and struggles of different identity groups can foster empathy and cultural competency. Students can become more aware of the challenges faced by others and the importance of inclusivity.

The following epigrams underscore the significant role that a course on identity politics can play in enhancing students' personal and intellectual growth, while fostering a deeper understanding of social science disciplines.

"The personal is political."—the foundational feminist slogan attributed to activist Carol Hanisch challenges the division between the private and public spheres, and suggests that issues like domestic violence, reproductive rights and workplace discrimination are not just personal problems but are linked to broader societal norms, laws and power dynamics. This catchphrase also suggests that individuals' experiences are influenced by larger structures of power, such as patriarchy, racism, classism and heteronormativity.

Understanding that personal issues have political dimensions can raise consciousness and foster solidarity and collective action.

"Identity is not found, but created."—this phrase, which was popularized by the writer and editor Dorothea Brande, underscores the dynamic, fluid, diverse, plural, and socially and culturally constructed nature of identity. It highlights the ways that identities are shaped by power structures and social hierarchies and the active role that individuals play in shaping their identities through their choices and interactions with others.

"We are not what other people say we are. We are who we know ourselves to be ..."—the words of actress and transgender activist Laverne Cox challenge the external imposition of identities and advocate for a self-defined understanding of who we are. In particular, this statement validates the lived experiences of transgender people and asserts that their self-identified gender is what truly defines them, rather than the gender assigned at birth or perceived by others.

"Identity shapes reality."—this statement captures the idea that our identities profoundly influence how we perceive, experience and engage with the world. It implies that identities act as cognitive filters through which we interpret the world and assign meaning to our experiences, and that the frameworks and schemas we develop based on our identities influence our roles, norms, expectations and communication and behavioral styles.

The study of identities is far from navel gazing; it addresses real-world issues. In fact, understanding how identities are constructed, experienced and intersect with social structures is crucial for addressing a host of pressing social issues.

By understanding how identities intersect with institutional and power structures, researchers can identify how class, gender and race affect access to resources, opportunities and life outcomes, and inform policies to address the root causes of inequality.

Studying identities can reduce stereotypes and prejudice and foster cross-cultural competency by promoting empathy and understanding of diverse experiences. This is crucial in multicultural societies where social cohesion depends on mutual respect and recognition.

Also, the study of identities gives voice to marginalized groups, highlighting their struggles and their campaigns to assert their rights.

So let me end with this thought: Through the lens of identity, social truths are revealed. This phrase suggests a basic truth: Examining society through the prism of identity provides critical insights into systemic inequalities, social norms, power dynamics and personal and collective experiences. It reveals how different identities experience varying levels of privilege or oppression and exposes how power is distributed and maintained.

The study of identity is a key to understanding society. Let's not forgo the insights it offers.

Viewpoint 4

> *"In actuality, 'woke' is a decades-old, sometimes casually used, bit of Black American vernacular. But given its widespread, often lazy interjection in political, cultural and ironic use cases today, 'woke' has both too many definitions and nowhere near enough examples that elevate it, or at least cushion it, in fair context."*

What Does It Mean to Be "Woke"?

Rachel Koning Beals

As this viewpoint by Rachel Koning Beals points out, there is no word more identified with identity politics than "woke." It is also a highly controversial term in the modern era. Koning Beals attempts to define it in this viewpoint by citing a book on the subject and describing the political backlash against what is known as "wokeism." She also explains that the origins of "woke" and "wokeism" extend back far earlier than the current era, offering historical context for the concept. Rachel Koning Beals is a news editor for MarketWatch based in Chicago.

"'Woke' is being used to describe everything and nothing. What does it actually mean?" by Rachel Koning Beals, MarketWatch, March 20, 2023. Reprinted by permission.

As you read, consider the following questions:

1. Why is "woke" an example of language appropriation and cultural appropriation, according to this viewpoint?
2. What is cancel culture? What is its relationship to "woke" as explained in this viewpoint?
3. According to this viewpoint, why has there been such a backlash against woke culture?

Easily, or perhaps coherently, defining this four-letter word—which feels even shorter when stripped of vital context—stumped a political commentator this week.

Bethany Mandel had even co-written a book on "wokeism" and what she believes is the negative influence of far-left politics on children in American schools. Mandel, a conservative cultural commentator and columnist whose Twitter profile says she homeschools, titled that book *Stolen Youth: How Radicals Are Erasing Innocence and Indoctrinating a Generation*.

But after Mandel herself suggested in a web interview with *The Hill*'s "Rising" that many African Americans "consider themselves liberal, but fewer consider themselves woke," she struggled to answer when co-host Briahna Joy Gray asked her to define what "woke" means to her. And that struggle went viral.

Mandel, suggesting that on-air jitters and the sleep deprivation of a working mom with young kids played a part, later tweeted her book's definition.

In actuality, "woke" is a decades-old, sometimes casually used, bit of Black American vernacular. But given its widespread, often lazy interjection in political, cultural and ironic use cases today, "woke" has both too many definitions and nowhere near enough examples that elevate it, or at least cushion it, in fair context.

Or is it simply that "woke" is a tidier natural evolution from "cancel culture" and "political correctness"?

There has been an official response in word world. The Oxford English Dictionary has extended the definition of "woke" as not only a verb but now an adjective.

"I wish it would just go away. Black people essentially stopped using 'woke' a while ago, unless maybe using it with a side-eye," photographer Jessica Kelley, the daughter of the late novelist and essayist William Kelley, told MarketWatch.

The senior Kelley, known for *A Different Drummer* and other works, addressed co-opted cultural language in a 1962 *New York Times* essay, "If You're Woke, You Dig It." In it, the then-Harlem-based author pointed out that much of what passed for "beatnik" slang ("dig," "chick," "cool") originated with African Americans.

"That piece was more prophetic, it turns out, than even my dad could have imagined," Kelley said in an interview. She recalled the author using the term maybe one additional time, in a novel, and in the context of a relationship, not politics.

To her, "woke" is perhaps just the latest, though admittedly widespread, example of language appropriation that is a subset of cultural appropriation. New users "make fun of it at first, ridicule it, and then it's part of the public language," she said. "Eventually, it's turned into something else and used out of context."

To a large extent, "woke" has been appropriated mostly by right-wing politicians and commentators to denote programs, policies and priorities they don't like, such as inclusive education—and, perhaps more surprisingly, actions by the Walt Disney Co. and even the FBI and the U.S. military.

There are variations on the word itself. At the Republican National Convention in 2020, Rep. Matt Gaetz, a Florida Republican, raised alarm over American "woketopians," grouping them with socialists and supporters of then–Democratic presidential candidate Joe Biden.

Florida Gov. Ron DeSantis, an anticipated Republican presidential contender in 2024, said earlier this year that his state would "never surrender to the 'woke' mob" as he said state pension-fund money would be removed from the world's largest fund firm,

BlackRock, to avoid environmental, social and governance, or ESG, investments. Texas Gov. Greg Abbott, a fellow Republican, has also publicly announced his desire to stop "a woke agenda" by ordering state agencies to eliminate diversity-driven hiring.

On some programs on Fox News, whose parent Fox Corp. shares common ownership with MarketWatch publisher Dow Jones's parent, News Corp, outrage over a purported "gas-stove ban" gave way to "woke" mobs coming to rip those appliances out of American homes. And as Wall Street reeled in recent days after the swift demise of Silicon Valley Bank—the biggest American bank failure since the 2008 financial meltdown—some social-media users joined cable-news pundits in pinning the collapse on its socially aware, or "woke," agenda. It was a claim that prompted an Associated Press fact check.

On the political left, to be "woke" in modern terms means to identify as a staunch social-justice advocate but, in particular, one who is in sync with contemporary political concerns. True enough, someone might be labeled that way whether or not they ever claimed such a title.

As might be expected, defensiveness around "wokeness" invites ironic blowback. A 2020 Hulu comedy series—called, what else, *Woke*—attempted to deconstruct the identity politics behind its current use. But the series drew its own criticism for striking an outdated and too-centrist political viewpoint—that is, for not being "woke" enough, as Vox reported.

In fact, one of the term's earliest uses was in a historical recording of the protest song "Scottsboro Boys" by blues musician Lead Belly, about the 1930s trials of nine Black teens falsely accused of raping two white women. In that recording, it was used to describe staying aware of the potential for racist violence as a Black person in America.

The first time many younger people heard "woke" in its current context was likely during the ascent of the Black Lives Matter movement. In 2014 in Ferguson, Mo., citizens marched nightly to protest the death of Michael Brown, an unarmed Black teenager shot by a white police officer. As they did, social media included an urgency to "stay woke" against police actions and other threats.

It's also true that culture can be a conveyance of activism, and the other way around. Childish Gambino, the musical stage name of actor Donald Glover, used "woke" in the chorus of 2016's "Redbone," a song also featured in the 2017 horror film Get Out. And Erykah Badu sings of "staying woke" on "Master Teacher."

Jessica Kelley stressed her belief that it is important as a nation to keep alive linguistics studies and hold up cultural language, because a lack of understanding means we can use language to separate people and weaponize words.

In the 1940s and '50s, Americans, especially Black Americans, worked hard to remove all regional or colloquial accents, a practice more relaxed these days. But there's a great loss in stripping language of cultural significance and forcing change faster than organic, generational shifts might naturally allow.

Increasingly, there's been an effort to respect African American Vernacular English (AAVE), Kelley added. AAVE, an area of study and a form of linguistics with its own verbs and unique action verbs, derived from English, French, the many African languages and all the influences that shaped the way that the first enslaved Africans brought to the New World created language to bridge their own differences and seek refuge from oppression, she said.

As for "woke" and its legacy, "I've given up trying to correct people," Kelley told MarketWatch. "I mean, if I had a dollar for every time I see it on Twitter and could link to my dad's works—well, I'd be rich."

Periodical and Internet Sources Bibliography

The following articles have been selected to supplement the diverse views presented in this chapter.

Karen Brodkin, "The Origins of Identity Politics," *Tikkun,* Winter/Spring 2018. https://muse.jhu.edu/pub/4/article/692991/pdf.

Amy Chua, "How America's Identity Politics Went from Inclusion to Division," *The Guardian*, March 1, 2018. https://www.theguardian.com/society/2018/mar/01/how-americas-identity-politics-went-from-inclusion-to-division.

Richard E. Ebeling, "Identity Politics: The New Totalitarianism," *The Epoch Times*, October 26, 2018. https://www.theepochtimes.com/opinion/identity-politics-the-new-totalitarianism-2697132.

Alicia Garza, "Identity Politics: Friend or Foe?" Othering and Belonging Institute, September 24, 2019. https://belonging.berkeley.edu/identity-politics-friend-or-foe.

Mike Gonzalez, "Uncovering the Origins of Identity Politics," the Heritage Foundation, July 28, 2020. https://www.heritage.org/progressivism/commentary/uncovering-the-origins-identity-politics.

German Lopez, "The Battle Over Identity Politics, Explained." Vox, August 17, 2017. https://www.vox.com/identities/2016/12/2/13718770/identity-politics.

Frank Newport, "Identity Politics in Context," Gallup News, December 3, 2021. https://news.gallup.com/opinion/polling-matters/357812/identity-politics-context.aspx.

Adam Ramsay, "Culture Wars: What is Identity Politics?" OpenDemocracy, December 12, 2021. https://www.opendemocracy.net/en/culture-wars-identity-politics-and-the-fight-against-surveillance-capitalism/.

Satyabrat Sinha, "Ethnicity and Identity Politics," *Encyclopedia of Violence, Peace, and Conflict,* 2022. https://www.sciencedirect.com/science/article/abs/pii/B978012820195400251X.

Sông to Sea, "Everything You Think You Know About Identity Politics Is Wrong," *Plan A Magazine*, 2020. https://planamag.com/everything-you-think-you-know-about-identity-politics-is-wrong/.

OPPOSING VIEWPOINTS® SERIES

Chapter 2

Has the Media Negatively Shaped the Identity Politics Debate?

Chapter Preface

Never before has "the media" been used in more blanket statements. It has become a catch-all for complaints, particularly from right-leaning Americans who claim the mainstream media is biased toward the left in its coverage of news and events. This chapter delves into the impact the media has had in recent years on the perceptions of identity politics and on identity politics themselves.

It has been legitimately argued that nobody should place the media under one huge umbrella. After all, it takes on many forms, including electronic, social, cable, and print. There are thousands, perhaps millions of news media outlets worldwide. Some lean right, some lean left, some take centrist stances. Many do not count objectivity as a motivating force—though they make that claim. But others do try to maintain a standard of objectivity. Lumping all media together is a convenient way to make claims to arguments that fit one's own narrative or political beliefs.

But despite this, the media has certainly shaped opinions surrounding identity politics. What is often derisively called the "mainstream media" has received the most criticism in recent years. Those are mostly newspapers perceived as left leaning, such as *The Washington Post* and *The New York Times* and cable news outlets such as MSNBC, and CNN. Those who rail against wokeism and left-wing identity politics point accusing fingers at those media sources as spewers of lies and divisive rhetoric.

This chapter touches upon how the media has indeed played a role in creating an atmosphere of political polarization in the United States and looks into possible solutions. It cites various kinds of media outlets, not just cable and print news, that have grown particularly controversial. It cites social media as perhaps the worst offender because it reaches almost everyone and it allows people to perpetuate their own viewpoints on any social or political issue and express their opinions on identity politics, wokeism, and other subjects in often incendiary ways without experiencing the guilt associated with insulting others face-to-face.

The print, online, and cable media does decide on which stories to cover, to what extent they are covered, and, if not totally objective, what political slant to apply to this coverage. Those on the right of the political spectrum complained vehemently in particular about the mainstream media's reaction to the coverage of the protests and riots that followed the murder of Black American George Floyd in 2020 and the flourishing of the Black Lives Matter movement that resulted. But social media has been blamed more for other identity politics issues, such as the greater sensitivity demanded by some for LGBTQ+ rights.

This chapter delves deeply into how both traditional and social media have impacted polarization on issues related to identity politics and the perception of slanted coverage that perpetuates that polarization.

Viewpoint 1

> *"Since the 1950s, social psychologists have tried to understand what pits groups against each other—and today, they're applying these insights to figure out what is happening in the United States."*

Media Is Just One Factor in Polarization

Lee de-Wit, Sander van der Linden, and Cameron Brick

Citing research that suggests political polarization has been driven in part by identifying with a particular political group (such as a party or organization), this viewpoint examines the results and suggests processes and solutions to fix these problems. It seeks to explain the morality of making changes on issues such as gun control and citizenship for the children of undocumented immigrants while bringing people together for a common purpose. The authors assert that many Americans tend to agree on policy issues, but are divided by political identity. Lee de-Wit is a lecturer in political psychology at Cambridge University in the United Kingdom. Sander van der Linden is an assistant professor of social psychology and director of the Cambridge Social Decision-Making Lab at the University of Cambridge. Cameron Brick is a social psychologist who studies how people react to shared dilemmas such as political polarization or climate change using surveys and experiments.

"What Are the Solutions to Political Polarization?" by Lee de-Wit, Sander van der Linden, and Cameron Brick, The Greater Good Magazine, July 2, 2019. Reprinted by permission.

As you read, consider the following questions:

1. According to this viewpoint, what fraction of Americans support stricter gun laws?
2. When did social psychologists start studying political polarization?
3. What solutions to political polarization do the authors offer?

What drives political polarization? Is it simply disagreement over the great issues of the day? Not necessarily. Recent research by the More in Common Foundation found that more than three-fourths of Americans support both stricter gun laws and a pathway to citizenship for undocumented immigrants brought here as children. Roughly the same number of Americans agree "that our differences are not so great that we cannot come together."

Are They Right?

The More in Common results could be interpreted to suggest that we can build bipartisan support for specific policies by focusing more on their boring nuts and bolts. Unfortunately, however, voters don't evaluate policies in isolation. Research has highlighted that people actively use partisan cues when evaluating different policies.

For example, a study by Carlee Beth Hawkins and Brian Nosek shows that labeling policies as "Democrat" or "Republican" can influence policy support, depending on the implicit bias of participants toward each party. A 2017 study by David Tannenbaum and colleagues finds that support for policy "nudges"—such as changing 401k retirement accounts to opt-out rather than opt-in—was heavily influenced by whether they were framed as supporting the goals of the Democratic or Republican party. This was true of regular U.S. citizens and for senior government leaders. Similarly, a 2018 study by Leaf Van Boven and colleagues finds that the majority of Republicans agree that climate change is happening—but their support for policy solutions declined when presented by Democrats.

In other words, people like policies proposed by members of their own in-group—and they don't like ideas generated by out-groups. This dynamic is not new. Since the 1950s, social psychologists have tried to understand what pits groups against each other—and today, they're applying these insights to figure out what is happening in the United States. This research doesn't provide definitive answers, but it does suggest some potential solutions, from changes to the voting system to the development of common goals that might enable groups to work together.

How Morality Becomes Partisan

The More in Common report illustrates that some of the most divisive topics often involve deep moral beliefs. For example, different political groups are very polarized on beliefs about responsibility, such as "people's outcomes in life are determined largely by forces outside of their control," or "people are largely responsible for their own outcomes in life." Similarly, liberals and conservatives are very divided on questions of whether parenting should focus on cultivating a child's curiosity versus good manners, or independence versus respect for elders.

In a new study published this year, Annemarie S. Walter and David P. Redlawsk directly pitted people's moral concerns with their partisan identity. They presented 2,000 participants with examples of different moral violations by different actors. Based on previous research, Walter and Redlawsk had thought that the nature of the moral violation might be the most significant factor in people's evaluations, as there are reasons to think that liberals and conservatives are concerned with some moral violations more than others. What they found, however, is that it wasn't the nature of the moral violation that was most important. Instead, it was the political allegiance of the violator. Democrats in the study were prone to giving Democrats a pass; the same was even more true of Republicans.

This partisan influence on policy preferences and moral judgments is a cause for both hope and concern. On one hand, it reiterates a point made by Daniel Yudkin in a *New York Times* op-ed about the More in Common report: that the U.S. may actually be less politically polarized based on certain moral or policy issues—at least when there aren't clear partisan associations. On the other hand, it highlights that as soon as a moral or political issue becomes associated with a particular party, it can become polarizing.

This is why it increasingly feels like U.S. politics has entered into a vicious cycle, whereby the moral and emotional language used to galvanize one side is directly antagonizing the other. The us-and-them nature of the debate has led to such a breakdown of trust that even hearing a policy proposed by the other side can be enough to trigger opposition to that policy. New policies (whatever their merit) can therefore quickly become symbols of conflict for the two sides to rally around.

What Are the Solutions?

This suggests that while there might be various political seeds that have helped drive the recent spike in polarization, it has gotten to a point where polarization is being exacerbated by some of the psychological processes that shape how we interpret identity and groups. This is a significant point to understand because it highlights that if we are to address polarization, we need to think not just about political solutions, but also solutions that are grounded in our understanding of social psychology.

1. Intergroup Contact

The "contact hypothesis" suggests that getting to know each other can reduce prejudice between groups. However, social contact can be done well and done badly. As we discussed in a previous article, following political opponents on Twitter can make people more extreme in their political views. It turns out that many conditions have to be met for contact to reduce prejudice, including having contact be sustained, with more than one member of the group, including a genuine exchange of ideas, and between individuals of similar social rank. These conditions have been very difficult to meet in designing social policies.

One promising civic model for enabling more meaningful contact between groups in conflict involves "Citizens Assemblies," where representative citizens are brought together to deliberate over challenging social or political issues. These assemblies can be thought of as a kind of jury duty for political deliberation, and they offer a platform for different groups to discuss issues in a way that can highlight where common ground exists and how it can be acted upon.

For example, Ireland has run several Citizens Assembles since 2016 that made policy recommendations that have been credited with advances in Ireland's approach to climate change. Indeed, participants in a recent Citizens Assembly on Brexit, run by Alan Renwick and colleagues at University College London, came to a compromise that could resolve the current impasse surrounding the U.K.'s decision to leave the European Union.

2. Perspective Taking

Perhaps one of the most important aspects of contact is that it might enable one to see things from another's perspective. The promise of perspective taking was recently illustrated in an experiment to attempt to change support for issues faced by transgender minorities. In this intervention, a brief exchange exploring a range of issues from the perspective of a trans individual was sufficient to shift people's attitudes on this controversial topic. Indeed, the attitude change seemed to persist even six months later, which is unusual for brief psychological interventions.

In his book *The Better Angels of Our Nature*, Pinker argues that the printing press may have had an important role in increasing levels of empathy following the Enlightenment by making it easier to read stories framed in the perspective of others. Indeed, Pinker speculates that some of the literature written from the perspective of Black slaves may have been instrumental to the abolition of slavery.

Considering the revolution in communication technology in our lifetimes, social media may have done more to promote taking sides than seeing the world through the eyes of another. Social media companies, and the governments that regulate them, clearly need to reflect on the extent to which these platforms encourage "side taking" instead of "perspective taking."

3. Superordinate Goals

One of the clearest solutions from the psychological literature is that identity-based conflicts require common goals or a "superordinate" sense of identity to bring people back together. In other words, we need a large sense of ourselves that is able to bridge smaller differences. This need to create a superordinate identity has clearly been intuitive to rulers for centuries, who would use various traditions and ceremonies to help build alliances between different countries and cultures.

Of course, superordinate goals also come with a potential risk. Whenever we form an in-group, we also create out-groups. As Richard Dawkins recently tweeted:

> National pride has evil consequences. Prefer pride in humanity. German pride gave us Hitler, American pride gave us Trump, British pride gave us Brexit. If you must have pride, be proud that *Homo sapiens* could produce a Darwin, Shakespeare, Mandela, Einstein, Beethoven.

Unfortunately, drawing a parallel between Trump and Hitler is perhaps itself an illustration of the polarized nature of modern discourse. Dawkins does have a point, however: The use of a superordinate identity such as American or European has potential risks. So, should we just think of ourselves as humans—or is the idea of "humanity" too abstract? Former British prime minister Theresa May famously criticized such a universalist perspective, stating: "If you believe you are a citizen of the world, you are a citizen of nowhere."

Is that true? Research suggests that a universalist perspective might well have underappreciated benefits. Sam McFarland

and colleagues recently reviewed this topic and found that those who identify highly as citizens of the world are indeed more empathic. Of course, those who are more empathic might simply identify more as international citizens. This idea warrants further testing, particularly as McFarland and colleagues identify several factors that might serve to further develop this sense of international citizenship.

4. Proportional Voting

While searching for psychological solutions to polarization, it's important not to ignore the context in which political decisions are made, and to think about the way in which different political systems will engage with, and exacerbate, aspects of our psychology.

The U.S. is one of the few countries to be dominated by just two political parties. This fact is almost certainly a reflection of the "winner take all"/"first past the post" voting system. Many countries employ a proportional (or mixed) system, which means that if a party gets 5 percent of the popular vote, they will receive 5 percent of the seats in a given representative body. In the U.S., this party would almost certainly get no representation—which could worsen the us-and-them dynamic of the U.S. political system.

For now, however, there isn't systematic evidence comparing the extent of identity-based politics with the political system used in the U.S. Unfortunately, that kind of large-scale, cross-country research is often the most difficult to obtain, but could be exactly what we need to understand how different voting systems might influence polarization.

That said, there is evidence that more proportional systems have higher levels of voter turnout (at least for supporters of smaller parties). In turn, that increase in turnout is correlated with citizens being more likely to report feeling that their vote makes a difference. This doesn't necessarily stop politics becoming less polarized, but it might make it harder for the extremes to come to dominate.

5. Voting for Policies, Not for Parties

Another potential solution to identity-based policy preferences is to hold direct referendums on specific issues. Among large territories, California and Switzerland both regularly use referendums to address complex policy topics. Referendums are used less frequently in other countries to try to resolve controversial topics, as was the case with gay marriage in Australia or voting reform in New Zealand. When designed well, referendums might cut across existing partisan divides, and if a clear majority is reached, they can signal a new social norm that can help a country move forward.

For those who are familiar with the fallout from the recent Brexit referendum in the U.K., however, this suggestion would probably seem a little laughable. Contemptuous, even. Indeed, there is evidence that the referendum in the U.K. has itself spilled over into a new form of emotional polarization, as recent data from YouGov highlights that (especially younger) "Remain" supporters would not want to see a close relative marry a "Leaver" (a member of the opposing political camp). There's another problem as well: While Australians did indeed vote to legalize same-sex marriage, it could have gone the other way; allowing the majority to vote on the civil and human rights of a minority is very risky.

Like many complex political systems, however, referendums can be designed well and designed badly. In countries with more established systems of direct democracy, the U.K. referendum wouldn't have even been legal. For example, in Switzerland, referendums have to be about precisely defined changes to the law, not vaguely defined outcomes. In New Zealand's referendum on the voting system, an independent educational body was created to inform both sides of the debate without taking a position (as the British government controversially did during the Brexit referendum).

The psychological impact of more direct voting systems is worthy of further enquiry. When poorly implemented, referendums risk causing new fault lines along which polarization can manifest. When well implemented, referendums might cut across existing lines of polarization and help establish a new social norm that can move a country forward.

From reframing issues to tap into a superordinate sense of identity, to promoting forms of contact that encourage perspective taking, social psychology does offer some useful ideas for thinking about how to tackle polarization. Furthermore, social psychology provides insights into the potential implications of different kinds of voting systems and the way in which they might exacerbate or diminish identity-based politics. As we have been careful to try and illustrate, however, experiments in social psychology do not yield off-the-shelf solutions that would be effective in all political contexts. Nevertheless, the farther that modern politics sinks into a self-fulfilling cycle of identity-based polarization, the more we'll need new insights from social science.

Viewpoint 2

> *"Besides being more politically siloed on average, our research found that TV news consumers are much more likely than web consumers to maintain the same partisan news diets over time."*

Cable News Has a Greater Impact on Political Identity and Polarization than Social Media

Homa Hosseinmardi

According to this viewpoint by Homa Hosseinmardi, while social media has largely been blamed for growing polarization in recent years, cable news media has a greater impact on increasing polarization and solidifying political identities. This is because a large percentage of American adults still consume the news through television, and because news channels have become politically polarized, viewers can choose to only watch channels that align with their own political identity. Because of this, people who get their news from TV are not exposed to opposing political perspectives, which allows them to develop more rigid political identities. Homa Hosseinmardi is an associate research scientist in computational social science at the University of Pennsylvania.

"Don't Be Too Quick to Blame Social Media for America's Polarization—Cable News Has a Bigger Effect, Study Finds," by Homa Hosseinmardi (University of Pennsylvania), The Conversation, August 10, 2022, https://theconversation.com/dont-be-too-quick-to-blame-social-media-for-americas-polarization-cable-news-has-a-bigger-effect-study-finds-187579. Licensed under CC BY-ND 4.0 International.

As you read, consider the following questions:

1. According to the data cited in this viewpoint, what percentage of Americans are politically polarized because of their TV news consumption?
2. What counterintuitive finding does Hosseinmardi cite from the research?
3. According to this viewpoint, why is it important to be exposed to opposing political perspectives?

The past two election cycles have seen an explosion of attention given to "echo chambers," or communities where a narrow set of views makes people less likely to challenge their own opinions. Much of this concern has focused on the rise of social media, which has radically transformed the information ecosystem.

However, when scientists investigated social media echo chambers, they found surprisingly little evidence of them on a large scale—or at least none on a scale large enough to warrant the growing concerns. And yet, selective exposure to news does increase polarization. This suggested that these studies missed part of the picture of Americans' news consumption patterns. Crucially, they did not factor in a major component of the average American's experience of news: television.

To fill in this gap, I and a group of researchers from Stanford University, the University of Pennsylvania and Microsoft Research tracked the TV news consumption habits of tens of thousands of American adults each month from 2016 through 2019. We discovered four aspects of news consumption that, when taken together, paint an unsettling picture of the TV news ecosystem.

TV Trumps Online

We first measured just how politically siloed American news consumers really are across TV and the web. Averaging over the four years of our observations, we found that roughly 17% of Americans are politically polarized—8.7% to the left and 8.4%

to the right—based on their TV news consumption. That's three to four times higher than the average percentage of Americans polarized by online news.

Moreover, the percentage of Americans polarized via TV ranged as high as 23% at its peak in November 2016, the month in which Donald Trump was elected president. A second spike occurred in the months leading into December 2018, following the "blue wave" midterm elections in which a record number of Democratic campaign ads were aired on TV. The timing of these two spikes suggests a clear connection between content choices and events in the political arena.

Staying in TV Echo Chambers

Besides being more politically siloed on average, our research found that TV news consumers are much more likely than web consumers to maintain the same partisan news diets over time: after six months, left-leaning TV audiences are 10 times more likely to remain segregated than left-leaning online audiences, and right-leaning audiences are 4.5 times more likely than their online counterparts.

While these figures may seem intimidating, it is important to keep in mind that even among TV viewers, about 70% of right-leaning viewers and about 80% of left-leaning viewers do switch their news diets within six months. To the extent that long-lasting echo chambers do exist, then, they include only about 4% of the population.

Narrow TV Diets

Partisan segregation among TV audiences goes even further than left- and right-leaning sources, we found. We identified seven broad buckets of TV news sources, then used these archetypes to determine what a typical unvaried TV news diet really looks like.

We found that, compared to online audiences, partisan TV news consumers tend not to stray too far from their narrow sets of preferred news sources. For example, most Americans who consume mostly MSNBC rarely consume news from any other source besides CNN. Similarly, most Americans who consume mostly Fox News Channel do not venture beyond that network at all. This finding contrasts with data from online news consumers, who still receive sizable amounts of news from outside their main archetype.

What Is Political Identity?

What does it mean to think of yourself as "American" or "Peruvian"? What makes someone identify as "conservative" or "progressive"? How does one's gender, ethnic, religious, or class identity influence their political identity? How does politics influence our sense of our gender, ethnic, religious and class identity? These questions are complex, intertwined and important. Our sense of self [our identity] influences our politics and politics influences our sense of self [our identity].

What Are the Components of Political Identity?

Political identity is how a person or group of persons think of themselves in relation to the politics and government of a country. Everything that makes up our sense of self are components of our political identity. This includes our ethnicity, religion, gender, class, ideology, nationality and even our age and generation.

Why Is Political Identity Important in Studying Comparative Politics?

Understanding how individuals and groups see their own identity as it relates to politics and the state [government] is critical to the analysis of the political culture and political system of any country. In the United States, for example, there is a tendency to think of White evangelicals as likely to affiliate with the Republican Party and for Persons of Color to be more likely to affiliate with the Democratic Party. People with different political identities might also have different ideas of what it means to be "patriotic" or even "American". Identity

continued on next spread

can be the driving force behind a social or political movement. Identity also can be the goal of a social or political movement in terms of gaining acceptance or redefining traditional identities (Bernstein, 2005).

What Is Identity Politics?

What Is "Identity Politics" and How Is That Different from "Political Identity"?

The term identity politics refers to the "tendency for people of a particular religion, race, social background, etc., to form exclusive political alliances, moving away from traditional broad-based party politics" (Lexico, n.d.). While identity politics can provide a sense of belonging and purpose for a group of people, it also can lead to division and a sense of "us" versus "them". If the sense of belonging and membership in one group outweighs the sense of belonging and membership in a broader group, it can become more difficult for a society to address issues facing all people in the country.

"What is Political Identity?" by Dino Bozonelos, Julia Wendt, Charlotte Lee, Jessica Scarffe, Masahiro Omae, Josh Franco, Byran Martin, and Stefan Veldhuis, The LibreTexts.

Distilling Partisanship

Finally, we found an imbalance between partisan TV news channels and the broader TV news environment. Our observations revealed that Americans are turning away from national TV news generally in substantial numbers—and crucially, this exodus is more from centrist news buckets than from left- or right-leaning ones. Within the remaining TV news audience, we found movement from broadcast news to cable news, trending toward MSNBC and Fox News.

Together, these trends reveal a counterintuitive finding: Although the overall TV news audience is shrinking, the partisan TV news audience is growing. This means that the audience as a whole is in the process of being "distilled"—remaining TV viewers are growing increasingly partisan, and the partisan proportion of TV news consumers is on the rise.

Why It Matters

Exposure to opposing views is critical for functional democratic processes. It allows for self-reflection and tempers hostility toward political outgroups, whereas only interacting with similar views in political echo chambers makes people more entrenched in their own opinions. If echo chambers truly are as widespread as recent attention has made them out to be, it can have major consequences for the health of democracy.

Our findings suggest that television—not the web—is the top driver of partisan audience segregation among Americans. It is important to note that the vast majority of Americans still consume relatively balanced news diets.

However, given that the partisan TV news audience alone consumes more minutes of news than the entire online news audience, it may be worth devoting more attention to this huge and increasingly politicized part of the information ecosystem.

Viewpoint 3

> *"Online users who feel strongly about a topic will post about it using strong language, such as 'white privilege.' This language will get people riled up toward one side or another."*

Strong Language Increases Polarization on Social Media

Christopher Quarles

In this viewpoint, Christopher Quarles discusses how using charged language in political social media posts can increase polarization and decrease the number of productive conversations. In particular, Quarles' research focuses on the use of "white privilege" and how it can drive some people away from supporting racial equality in online conversations. Using terms like "white privilege" that cause a strong emotional reaction results in more anger and extremism in social media. According to Quarles, this is because "white privilege" creates an "us vs. them" mentality and causes people to identify more with their social group and become closed off to concepts they may otherwise support. At the time this viewpoint was published, Christopher Quarles was a PhD candidate in information at the University of Michigan School of Information.

"Use of 'White Privilege' Makes Online Discussions More Polarized and Less Constructive," Christopher Quarles (University of Michigan), The Conversation, May 11, 2022, https://theconversation.com/use-of-white-privilege-makes-online-discussions-more-polarized-and-less-constructive-181013. Licensed under CC BY-ND 4.0 International.

As you read, consider the following questions:

1. According to the study cited in this viewpoint, what percent of white people surveyed became ambivalent or hostile to the idea of renaming college buildings when "white privilege" was used in the question?
2. What impact does the use of strong language have on people who would be good mediators or otherwise have a more moderate perspective?
3. What is social identity?

A wide variety of historical, economic and cultural forces combine to allow a larger percentage of whites to climb up the socioeconomic ladder than Blacks and Hispanics.

Some people call the combined effects of these forces "white privilege." Though these words are commonly used, research by Lia Bozarth and me has found that use of "white privilege" on social media can actually decrease support for racially progressive policies.

We found that the term can increase online political polarization and lead to lower quality conversations on social media. In particular, the term drives some whites who would otherwise support efforts toward racial equality away from online conversations.

Effects of Using 'White Privilege'

In the past decade there has been a push on college campuses to re-title buildings named after people involved with slavery or discrimination.

We used the issue of renaming these buildings as a way to examine how language affects online conversations.

We recruited 924 U.S. residents from Amazon's Mechanical Turk for our experiment. Half of the research participants were given a social media post containing the following question: "Should colleges rename buildings that were named after people who actively supported racial inequality?"

The other half saw an identical question, except the term "racial inequality" was swapped with "white privilege." We randomly chose which half received each question.

This random assignment allowed us to show causality—and gave us confidence that the choice of language created the effects we saw.

We asked the participants to respond to their question, and also measured how likely they were to engage with the post in the first place. We then focused on the set of people who were likely to engage with that post online.

The term "white privilege" had two effects.

The first was to decrease the quality of conversation among both whites and non-whites. There were more comments that insulted people, attacked the question itself or simply made no sense.

The second effect was to make the set of responses less supportive of renaming the buildings—and more polarized.

The people who were asked about racial inequality were, on average, very supportive. Those who thought it was a good idea to rename college buildings outnumbered opponents more than 2-to-1.

But the group that was asked about "white privilege" was strongly divided, with just as many opponents as supporters. This shift was caused completely by a change in some whites.

Use of "white privilege" caused 50% of whites who would have been supportive to become ambivalent or hostile. We don't know which half would have changed their minds. But, due to the experimental design, we can be confident they were there.

In addition, we found that many of the supportive whites just chose to avoid the conversation altogether. While they might have expressed their support for stopping racial inequality, they wouldn't join a conversation about white privilege.

Because the terms "white privilege" and "racial inequality" have different meanings, we performed an extra analysis to understand what caused these effects.

What we found was consistent with other research suggesting a process called motivated reasoning.

In this experiment, the different meanings of the terms "white privilege" and "racial inequality" didn't seem to directly affect how people reasoned about renaming buildings.

Instead, we found evidence that the difference in language first affected whether they were supportive of renaming buildings. Only after deciding on an opinion did they find reasons to support it.

Polarization or Misunderstanding?

Our results offer insight into one mechanism underlying the polarization and vitriol we see on social media.

Online users who feel strongly about a topic will post about it using strong language, such as "white privilege."

This language will get people riled up toward one side or another. And the people who might be good mediators—such as supportive whites in our study—are less likely to engage.

The people who remain are then more likely to share extreme views. They create online posts, and the cycle continues.

The result is social media dominated by outrage and extremism, rather than respectful discourse.

Some people I've talked to have been genuinely surprised by these results. Others thought they were obvious and not even worth researching.

This is notable, because it suggests that some of the conflict we see online is not caused by malice, but by a lack of understanding.

Social Identity Dynamics

In our study, the term "white privilege" changed the behavior of some whites. But the psychology behind this change is common to all humans. In fact, the psychological research that first examined this effect focused on Blacks' performance in school.

The term "white privilege" taps into a deep-seated tendency as old as humanity.

As social creatures, humans are naturally inclined to split the world into "us" and "them." This can lead to thinking of others—and sometimes ourselves—as a stereotypical member of our group.

Further, we are members of multiple groups simultaneously, according to our age, profession, race, politics and family roles. At any given moment, social cues affect which group is the most forefront in our minds.

This natural tendency to view ourselves through a social identity allowed Germanic tribes who had been warring with each other to band together to drive back invading Romans.

It enabled whites to view Blacks as inferior throughout much of American history and led some Blacks to agree with that view.

It played a role in anti-Muslim sentiment after 9/11.

It's involved in political partisanship and in protests against authoritarian regimes.

And it's one reason we feel more comfortable in a group of people like ourselves.

Phrases like "white privilege" play on this reasoning by implying that all whites are similar and have the same negative traits.

Unsurprisingly, the accusation—even subtly implied—that everyone in your race is "bad" can create strong reactions. Some people will just disregard the speaker entirely.

But many others will feel intense visceral emotions such as anger, which can lead us to be more confrontational, or shame, which can cause people to withdraw.

When faced with the term "white privilege," it's not surprising that some whites will look less favorably on the speaker's ideas. And it makes sense that the whites who are more sympathetic will tend to withdraw.

Of course this reaction, which psychologists call "social identity threat," is not unique to white people.

At some point in their lives, everyone feels unwelcome or devalued because of a group they identify as part of, whether that's being Black, white, Hispanic, young, old, female, male, Christian or atheist.

A Sticky Problem

Surveys show that an overwhelming majority of Americans think that everyone should get an equal shot at success, and numerous studies have shown that race is involved in economic opportunity and social mobility. While the data is clear that racial inequality persists in America, its causes are complex and have so far proven intractable.

Meanwhile, social media users spend their time attacking each other, giving the impression of an outraged and polarized citizenry.

Effective communication about personal topics like race can be challenging. The careful use of inclusive language is one way to gather public support—or at least promote meaningful discussion.

Words matter, and our research demonstrates how phrases like "white privilege" affect the way controversial issues on race are perceived.

Viewpoint 4

> *"Those at both the left and right ends of the spectrum, who together comprise about 20% of the public overall, have a greater impact on the political process than do those with more mixed ideological views."*

Media Habits Impact Political Polarization

Amy Mitchell, Jeffrey Gottfried, Jocelyn Kiley, and Katerina Eva Matsa

In this viewpoint, the authors focus on how the media fuels polarization in modern society. The view here is that people feel allegiance to news sources that reaffirm their opinions rather than clicking on or reading a variety of outlets to gain as much insight as possible and therefore base their views on greater knowledge. Amy Mitchell is former director of journalism research at Pew Research Center, where Jeffrey Gottfried is an associate director of research, Jocelyn Kiley is a senior associate director of research, and Katerina Eva Matsa is director of news and information research.

As you read, consider the following questions:

1. How does the impact of people on either end of the political spectrum compare to the impact of people with more mixed views? Why is this the case?

"Political Polarization & Media Habits" by Amy Mitchell, Jeffrey Gottfried, Jocelyn Kiley, and Katerina Eva Matsa, Pew Research Center, October 21, 2014.

2. How do the news consumption habits of conservatives compare to those of liberals?
3. According to this viewpoint, why are there more media outlets that slant politically left instead of right?

When it comes to getting news about politics and government, liberals and conservatives inhabit different worlds. There is little overlap in the news sources they turn to and trust. And whether discussing politics online or with friends, they are more likely than others to interact with like-minded individuals, according to a new Pew Research Center study.

The project—part of a year-long effort to shed light on political polarization in America—looks at the ways people get information about government and politics in three different settings: the news media, social media and the way people talk about politics with friends and family. In all three areas, the study finds that those with the most consistent ideological views on the left and right have information streams that are distinct from those of individuals with more mixed political views—and very distinct from each other.

These cleavages can be overstated. The study also suggests that in America today, it is virtually impossible to live in an ideological bubble. Most Americans rely on an array of outlets—with varying audience profiles—for political news. And many consistent conservatives and liberals hear dissenting political views in their everyday lives.

Yet as our major report on political polarization found, those at both the left and right ends of the spectrum, who together comprise about 20% of the public overall, have a greater impact on the political process than do those with more mixed ideological views. They are the most likely to vote, donate to campaigns and participate directly in politics. The five ideological groups in this analysis (consistent liberals, mostly liberals, mixed, mostly conservatives and consistent conservatives) are based on responses to 10 questions about a range of political values. That those who express consistently conservative or consistently liberal opinions have different ways of informing themselves about politics and government is not surprising. But the depth of these divisions—and the differences between those who have strong ideological views and those who do not—are striking.

Overall, the study finds that consistent conservatives:

- Are tightly clustered around a single news source, far more than any other group in the survey, with 47% citing Fox News as their main source for news about government and politics.
- Express greater distrust than trust of 24 of the 36 news sources measured in the survey. At the same time, fully 88% of consistent conservatives trust Fox News.
- Are, when on Facebook, more likely than those in other ideological groups to hear political opinions that are in line with their own views.
- Are more likely to have friends who share their own political views. Two-thirds (66%) say most of their close friends share their views on government and politics.

By contrast, those with consistently liberal views:

- Are less unified in their media loyalty; they rely on a greater range of news outlets, including some—like NPR and *The New York Times*—that others use far less.
- Express more trust than distrust of 28 of the 36 news outlets in the survey. NPR, PBS and the BBC are the most trusted news sources for consistent liberals.
- Are more likely than those in other ideological groups to block or "defriend" someone on a social network—as well as to end a personal friendship—because of politics.
- Are more likely to follow issue-based groups, rather than political parties or candidates, in their Facebook feeds.

Those with down-the-line conservative and liberal views do share some common ground; they are much more likely than others to closely follow government and political news. This carries over to their discussions of politics and government. Nearly four-in-ten consistent conservatives (39%) and 30% of consistent liberals tend to drive political discussions—that is, they talk about politics often, say others tend to turn to them for information rather than the reverse, and describe themselves as leaders rather than listeners in these kinds of conversations. Among those with mixed ideological views, just 12% play a similar role.

The Pew Research Center's American Trends Panel

Earlier this year, the Pew Research Center released a major analysis of changes in the American electorate titled Political Polarization in the American Public. The study, based on interviews with more than 10,000 adults nationwide, tracked the growing ideological consistency and partisan antipathy expressed by Americans, and how these views correlate with people's willingness to compromise, relationships with friends and family, and even preferences about where to live.

This report is based on a follow-up survey, about where people get political news and information, conducted among the 88% of panel members with online access. While the picture drawn might be slightly different if those without internet access had been included, this report provides a thorough look at political information consumption by the large online population.

It is important to note, though, that those at either end of the ideological spectrum are not isolated from dissenting views about politics. Nearly half (47%) of across-the-board conservatives—and 59% of across-the-board liberals — say they at least sometimes disagree with one of their closest political discussion partners.

For those closer to the middle of the ideological spectrum, learning about politics, or discussing it with friends and family, is a less of a focus. When they do follow politics, their main news sources include CNN, local TV and Fox News, along with Yahoo News and Google News, which aggregate stories from a wide assortment of outlets; these U.S. adults see more of a mix of views in social media and are less likely to be aware of their friends' political leanings.

This study, the latest in a series of reports on political polarization, is based on an online survey conducted March 19-April 29, 2014, with 2,901 members of the Pew Research Center's new American Trends Panel—a panel recruited from a telephone survey of 10,013 adults conducted earlier this year.

Among the key findings:

Media Sources: Nearly Half of Consistent Conservatives Cite Fox News

When it comes to choosing a media source for political news, conservatives orient strongly around Fox News. Nearly half of consistent conservatives (47%) name it as their main source for government and political news, as do almost a third (31%) of those with mostly conservative views. No other sources come close.

Consistent liberals, on the other hand, volunteer a wider range of main sources for political news—no source is named by more than 15% of consistent liberals and 20% of those who are mostly liberal. Still, consistent liberals are more than twice as likely as web-using adults overall to name NPR (13% vs. 5%), MSNBC (12% vs. 4%) and *The New York Times* (10% vs. 3%) as their top source for political news.

Among the large group of respondents with mixed ideological views, CNN (20%) and local TV (16%) are top sources; Fox News (8%), Yahoo News (7%) and Google News (6%) round out their top five sources.

Trust and Distrust: Liberals Trust Many, Conservatives Trust Few

At least as important as where people turn for news is whose news they trust. And here, the ideological differences are especially stark.

Respondents were asked whether they had heard of each of the 36 outlets listed in the accompanying graphic. For those they had heard of, they were asked about their trust—or distrust—in each source.

Liberals, overall, trust a much larger mix of news outlets than others do. Of the 36 different outlets considered, 28 are more trusted than distrusted by consistent liberals. Just eight earn higher shares of distrust than trust. Still, among those eight, the levels of distrust can be high: fully 81% of consistent liberals distrust Fox News, and 75% distrust *The Rush Limbaugh Show*.

Among consistent conservatives, by contrast, there are 24 sources that draw more distrust than trust. The same is true for 15 sources among those with mostly conservative views. And, of the eight outlets more trusted than distrusted by consistent conservatives, all but one, on balance, are distrusted by consistent liberals.

Also at play here is the degree to which people are more familiar with certain news sources than others. Some outlets such as CNN, ABC News and Fox News, are recognized by at least nine-in-ten respondents, meaning that more respondents offer a view of these outlets one way or the other. Outlets currently occupying more niche markets, such as Politico, the Economist or BuzzFeed, are known by only about a third of respondents. Thus, while they may elicit strong views in one direction, the share of respondents weighing in is relatively small.

This section of the report looks in detail at news audiences and trust and distrust of outlets across ideological groups.

Social Media: Conservatives More Likely to Have Like-Minded Friends

Consistent liberals who pay attention to politics on Facebook are also more likely than others to "like" or follow issue-based groups: 60% do this, compared with 46% of consistent conservatives and just a third (33%) of those with mixed views. And both the left and the right are more likely than others to follow political parties or elected officials: 49% of consistent conservatives and 42% of consistent liberals do so, compared with 29% of Facebook users overall.

Talking Politics: Dissenting Views Penetrate, but Less Frequently for the Ideologically Consistent

In personal conversations about politics, those on the right and left are more likely to largely hear views in line with their own thinking.

While only a quarter (25%) of respondents with mixed ideological views say most of their close friends share their own political views, that is true of roughly half (52%) of consistent liberals and two-thirds (66%) of consistent conservatives. And, when those who talk about politics are asked to name up to three people they most often talk to about politics, half (50%) of consistent conservatives name only individuals they describe as also being conservative—outpacing the 31% of consistent liberals who name only liberals.

At the same time, consistent liberals are more likely to stop talking to someone because of politics. Roughly a quarter (24%) have done so, compared with 16% of consistent conservatives and around 10% of those with more mixed political views.

Still, a solid portion of even the most ideologically aligned respondents encounter some political disagreement with their close discussion partners. Nearly half (47%) of consistent conservatives who talk about politics name one or more discussion partners with whom they disagree at least some of the time. This figure rises to more than half (59%) of consistent liberals and even larger shares of those with mostly liberal and ideologically mixed political views (79% each).

Media Outlets by the Ideological Composition of Their Audience

Ideological differences in media source preferences result in distinct audience profiles for many media outlets. Many sources, such as *The Wall Street Journal*, *USA TODAY*, ABC News, CBS News and NBC News have audiences that are, on average, ideologically similar to the average web respondent.

Reflecting liberals' use of a greater number of media sources, there are more outlets whose readers, watchers and listeners fall to the left of the average web respondent than to the right. At the same time, a handful of outlets have audiences that are more conservative than the average respondent.

Fox News sits to the right of the midpoint but is not nearly as far right as several other sources, such as the radio shows of Rush Limbaugh or Glenn Beck. A closer look at the audience breakdowns reveals why: While consistent conservatives get news from Fox News at very high rates, many of those with less conservative views also use Fox News. By contrast, the audiences for Limbaugh and Beck are overwhelmingly conservative.

By comparison, the average consumer of *The Wall Street Journal* sits very close to the typical survey respondent, but the range of *Journal* readers is far broader because it appeals to people on both the left and the right. As a result, while respondents overall cluster toward the center of the ideological spectrum, the *Journal*'s audience is relatively evenly distributed across the continuum: 20% are consistent liberals, 21% mostly liberal, 24% mixed, 22% mostly conservative and 13% consistent conservative.

Periodical and Internet Sources Bibliography

The following articles have been selected to supplement the diverse views presented in this chapter.

"Has Identity Politics Distracted Us From True Inclusion?" GZERO World, January 24, 2024. https://www.gzeromedia.com/gzero-world-clips/has-identity-politics-distracted-us-from-true-inclusion.

Karyn Amira and Alexander Abraham, "How the Media Uses the Phrase 'Identity Politics,'" *Political Science and Politics*, June 21, 2022. https://www.cambridge.org/core/journals/ps-political-science-and-politics/article/abs/how-the-media-uses-the-phrase-identity-politics/D7E1DAAF44BC572C0CA38DFC694D3B20.

EJ Antoni, "Media Elite Play Identity Politics While Americans Suffer From Fed's Monetary Moves," the Heritage Foundation, September 2, 2022. https://www.heritage.org/markets-and-finance/commentary/media-elite-play-identity-politics-while-americans-suffer-feds.

W. Lance Bennett, "The Personalization of Politics: Political Identity, Social Media and Changing Patterns of Participation," *The Annals of the American Academy of Political and Social Science*, November 2012. https://www.jstor.org/stable/23316140.

Adrianna Blackshire, "How Identity Politics Polarize Social Media Even Further," Democratic Erosion Consortium, June 10, 2022. https://www.democratic-erosion.com/2022/06/10/how-identity-politics-polarize-social-media-even-further/.

Ian Hawkins and Muniba Saleem, "How Social Media Use, Political Identity, and Racial Resentment Affect Perceptions of Reverse Racism in the United States," *Computers in Human Behavior*, September 2022. https://www.sciencedirect.com/science/article/abs/pii/S0747563222001595.

Diana Owen, "The New Media's Role in Politics," *MIT Technology Review*, March 11, 2019. https://www.technologyreview.com/2019/03/11/136690/the-new-medias-role-in-politics/?gad_source=1&gclid=Cj0KCQjwt4a2BhD6ARIsALgH7DoqrG0ypkAf9HxhrIljcEA5ErGSdi0Gs6O4Bo-uMSbqiFruM6j2qtMaAi38EALw_wcB.

Orestis Papakyriakopoulos and Ethan Zuckerman, "The Media During the Rise of Trump: Identity Politics, Immigration: 'Mexican' Demonization and Hate-Crime," *Proceedings of the International AAAI Conference on Web and Social Media*, May 22, 2021. https://ojs.aaai.org/index.php/ICWSM/article/view/18076.

Grace Sullivan, "Political Polarization, Identity Politics and Social Media," *The Observer*, November 11, 2022. https://www.ndsmcobserver.com/article/2022/11/political-polarization-identity-politics-and-social-media

Sanja Vico, "'Globalized Difference: Identity Politics on Social Media," *Journal of Global Diaspora & Media*, December 13, 2019. https://intellectdiscover.com/content/journals/10.1386/gdm_00004_1.

OPPOSING VIEWPOINTS® SERIES

CHAPTER 3

Are Identity Politics Effective in Creating Political Change?

Chapter Preface

Perhaps the question addressed in this chapter is not whether identity politics creates change, but whether it is positive or negative change. It is generally accepted that offering equal footing to all members of society—regardless of race, gender, sexuality, religion, and so on—is morally just. But many also contend that identity politics brings polarization that divides people.

The answer might be in the gray area in between. How can societies such as the United States and elsewhere around the world balance the push to ensure equality and opportunity among all their citizens without spurring resentment among other social identity groups? Can more be given to the marginalized without taking away from those who have historically been considered the privileged?

In either case the divisions created by identity politics and what has become known as rampant "wokeism" have grown acute and strengthened the political and social divides around the world—particularly in the United States. The debate surrounding the value of identity politics features one side that views identity politics as a necessary push to recognize and overcome the obstacles faced by marginalized people based on factors like color and sexual identity and the other side holding the belief that such campaigns were never necessary, or at least have gone overboard. It has become more heated in recent years.

Those arguments have infiltrated all levels of communication, including political rhetoric, various forms of traditional media, social media, and even at dinner tables that once held pleasant conversations about the daily lives of family members but have more recently become sites of tense discussions.

Terms such as identity politics, cancel culture, and wokeism have seeped into the American lexicon in modern times. Are they necessary components for transforming wrongs into rights for marginalized groups and correcting historical wrongs? Should we rid ourselves of historical figures who do not deserve to be venerated as heroes, such as by removing statues of slave owners and Confederate leaders? Or are these overcorrections to the marginalization that has impacted American society which will only bring about further division? Both sides of the debate are presented in these viewpoints.

Viewpoint 1

> *"Is amputation the best cure for this disease? The problem, of course, in submerging mementos of a painful past in the nearest body of water is things, especially painful things, have a tendency to re-emerge from the murky deep."*

Symbolic Representation Matters in Identity Politics

Kelly Grovier

In this viewpoint, Kelly Grovier discusses the destruction and dismantling of statues dedicated to Confederate military and political leaders as well as leaders with ties to the slave trade. These efforts to dismantle monuments to a racist past took off in the wake of the murder of George Floyd and the rise of the Black Lives Matter movement in 2020, and occurred in both the United Kingdom and the United Kingdom. Grovier explains that these monuments cause pain to historically marginalized and subjugated groups because they venerate their oppressors. However, Grovier argues that a better solution to these historical injustices would be to create memorials to those who were victims of these events to honor their strength and remind people of the injustices that have occurred. Kelly Grovier is a features correspondent for the BBC.

"Black Lives Matter protests: Why are statues so powerful?" by Kelly Grovier, BBC, June 12, 2020. Reprinted by permission.

As you read, consider the following questions:

1. Why did leaders on both sides of the political divide in the United Kingdom denounce the destruction of monuments?
2. According to Grovier, why do statues exist?
3. According to this viewpoint, how did Germany decide to address symbolic representations of the atrocities of the Nazi era? Does Grovier think this is effective?

What are statues for? The recent destruction of monuments in Britain and the U.S.—from the toppling in Bristol, England, last weekend of a bronze sculpture commemorating the 18th-Century British slave trader Edward Colston, to the defacement this week in Boston, Miami and Virginia of statues venerating Christopher Columbus and Confederate leaders—raises intriguing questions about the very purpose of public statuary. Why are we compelled to create such likenesses in the first place?

The defacements in the U.S. and the de-pedestaling of Colston, whose effigy was roughly rolled through the city streets by Black Lives Matter supporters before being dumped in a harbor, comes in the wake of the murder last month in Minneapolis, Minnesota, of an African-American, George Floyd, by a white police officer, who killed Floyd by kneeling on his neck. Floyd's slow eight-minute asphyxiation, captured on video by a passerby, has prompted passionate protests across the world and has added fresh urgency to campaigns demanding the removal of statues that glorify figures whose reputations (and fortunes) were built on the crushing of peoples of color and the stifling of Indigenous cultures.

In recent years, several monuments in the U.S. that commemorate military and political leaders of the defeated southern Confederacy (which fought to preserve slavery in the 1860s) have been dismantled or relocated, whisked away from public view. The fall of Colston in Britain is part of a fresh wave of expeditious extractions washing across the West. Earlier this week, Columbus was not only beheaded in Boston but torn down by ropes both in Minneapolis, Minnesota, and in Richmond, Virginia, where the 15th-century explorer's effigy was dragged to a nearby pond and drowned, Colston-style. A makeshift tombstone that read 'Racism, you will not be missed' was placed at the water's edge.

Fearing the acceleration of similar purges in the UK, leaders across the political spectrum raced to denounce the destruction of Colston's statue and to caution against the ripping down of any others. In a rare instance of synchronized messaging, the UK's Conservative Home Secretary Priti Patel and the leader of the opposition, Labour's Sir Keir Starmer, agreed that the attacks should be condemned, as thousands gathered in Oxford to demand the removal from Oriel College of a stone statue of Cecil Rhodes, a British supremacist who enriched himself by exploiting Africa's people and resources. At the time of writing, Rhodes' statue, which stares through a protective mesh like a captured beast, still teeters in the balance—inviting the world to reflect on what the appropriate fate for such relics of imperial plunder ought to be.

To answer that question, perhaps it's worth considering why statues exist in the first place and how we are hardwired to connect with them. The earliest-known material likeness of a human being, a small statuette of a female body discovered in a cave in Germany's Swabian Forest in 2008, may offer clues about the essence of our impulse to create such things. A mere 6cm (2.4in) in height and carved from woolly mammoth tusk 40,000 years ago, the so-called Venus of the Hohle Fels crudely exaggerates the features of a woman's body and is thought to have served as a fertility totem.

But it is not what the figurine, which demanded hundreds of hours of patient scraping to carve, depicts that is ultimately so revealing, but what it neglects to portray. The prehistoric

Identity Politics Is the Intersection of Politics and Social Science

Identity politics, political or social activity by or on behalf of a racial, ethnic, cultural, religious, gender, or other group, usually undertaken with the goal of rectifying injustices suffered by group members because of differences or conflicts between their particular identity (or misconceptions of their particular identity) and the dominant identity (or identities) of a larger society. Identity politics also aims, in the course of such activity, to eliminate negative misrepresentations (stereotypes) of particular groups that have served to justify their members' exclusion, exploitation, marginalization, oppression, or assimilation to the point of erasure. In a broad sense of the term, identity politics also encompasses nationalist or separatist movements within particular countries and territories. In the United States, groups associated with identity politics have included African Americans, Native Americans, Hispanic Americans, Asian Americans, Arab Americans, Muslims, Jews, feminists, and the LGBTQ community, among others. Identity politics is closely related to multiculturalism, or the general view that cultural minority groups deserve respectful acknowledgment of their distinctive belief systems, values, and ways of life.

Identity politics in the United States developed in the 1980s and '90s as a reaction to the perceived failure of liberal civil rights legislation

craftsman who slowly sculpted this hunk of ivory into shape made the extraordinary aesthetic decision to leave the object without a head. Where the neck should be, a small eye-hook loop, through which a string or strip of leather could be threaded, has been painstakingly sculpted. Dangling from a necklace, the statue's head is that of its wearer, who imaginatively completes the figurine by merging with it. From their earliest inception, in other words, statues were as much conceptual as they were material—less about the individuals they depict than about how we see ourselves.

> to eliminate identity-based inequities and injustices, such as racial and sexual discrimination. In the view of many leftist critics, liberal ideals of equality, such as equal rights, equality before the law, and equality of opportunity, were misguided and ultimately counterproductive, because their transcendent nature (their application to all persons, irrespective of identity) made it difficult in practice to justify policies designed to achieve greater social equity through direct assistance to historically oppressed and exploited groups, particularly African Americans. Indeed, during this period conservative activists and government officials frequently invoked the liberal value of "color blindness" to resist racial affirmative action programs in education, employment, government contracting, and other areas. A related criticism was that liberalism's emphasis on identity-independent equality rendered it capable of recognizing only the most overt and obvious identity-based injustices, not those that were relatively indirect, subtle, or systemic. Defenders of liberalism and other critics argued in response that the continued pursuit of identity politics had led to a fracturing of oppressed and exploited populations into numerous inward-looking interest groups whose differing priorities obscured their common goals and challenges and prevented the kind of mass mobilization necessary to secure their basic rights.
>
> **"Identity Politics: politics and social science" by Brian Duignan, Britannica.**

Just how engrained that instinct is—to perceive an aspect of oneself in the image of another—is impossible to measure. Such an impulse may explain why it is so agonizingly difficult to tolerate the persistence of memorials that venerate past masters of pain. Theirs is a suffocating weight. The outrage that many feel about having to share the streets with such hulking ghosts of oppression is deep and crushingly real. To address the thorny issue of how best to handle monuments whose aura an appreciable proportion of society finds toxic, countries have begun to adopt a variety of different strategies.

In London, the capital's mayor, Sadiq Khan, has announced the convening of a special commission to debate the dismantling (and erection) of the city's statues. In the U.S. on Wednesday, the speaker of the House of Representatives, Nancy Pelosi, hoping to pre-empt a violent plundering of Capitol Hill, called for the swift removal of 11 statues that commemorate Confederate leaders. "The statues in the Capitol should embody our highest ideals as Americans, expressing who we are and who we aspire to be as a nation," said the California Democrat in a statement, explaining her decision. "Monuments to men who advocated cruelty and barbarism to achieve such a plainly racist end are a grotesque affront to these ideals. Their statues pay homage to hate, not heritage. They must be removed."

Is amputation the best cure for this disease? The problem, of course, in submerging mementos of a painful past in the nearest body of water is things, especially painful things, have a tendency to re-emerge from the murky deep. The British street artist Banksy, whose own work routinely dredges the shallows of society's intolerance and forces us to confront uncomfortable shapes of hypocrisy and inequality, proposed this week an ingenious solution to the quandary that society finds itself in. "What should we do with the empty plinth in the middle of Bristol?", Banksy asked in a post on his Instagram account. "Here's an idea that caters for both those who miss the Colston statue and those who don't. We drag him out the water, put him back on the plinth, tie cable round his neck and commission some life size bronze statues of protestors in the act of pulling him down. Everyone happy. A famous day commemorated."

As Banksy's accompanying drawing (which wittily imagines a precariously repositioned Colston, faltering forever on the verge of collapse) suggests, what's tricky is finding the right balance when "catering" to the diverging perspectives of everyone in society who must bear the weight of a statue. In Germany, where decisions long ago had to be taken about how the Nazi era would be fossilized in the material memory of the nation's streets and squares, it was resolved that erasing the past was not an option. Rather than polluting the municipal air with monuments to the perpetrators of pain, however, efforts have been made to preserve instead memorials that honor the fortitude of Hitler's victims. Perhaps we should think of statues the way we think of trees. When one is found to be disfigured by disease we should resolve to plant a fresh copse, one that cleanses the atmosphere and doesn't choke our breath.

Viewpoint 2

> *"No matter what race, class or gender you are, you are human first."*

Have Identity Politics Gone Too Far?

Elias Williams

As Elias Williams argues in this viewpoint, even many liberals have decried the rise of "wokeism" and identity politics in recent years, claiming not only that it has been taken to an extreme but that it has resulted to some extent in the increased popularity of right-wing politicians because of reactionary responses to identity politics. Williams asserts that many aspects of identity politics are just superficial solutions to a deeper problem, and that deeming certain words unacceptable or statues inappropriate will not eliminate racism. Elias Williams is the founder of MANDEM, an online platform for men of color based in Bristol, United Kingdom.

As you read, consider the following questions:

1. How does Williams believe that generalizations impact identity politics?
2. Why does Williams think it is useful to have colonial memorabilia like statues around in the U.K.?
3. How does Williams believe identity should help people navigate the world?

"Has identity politics gone too far? My take" by Elias Williams, The Bristol Cable, February 21, 2019. Reprinted by permission.

In many ways the term "identity politics" is completely redundant. There is no such thing as a politics unaffected by identity. Everyone's political views are undeniably shaped by their own experiences. Today, the term identity politics seems to only be used when referring to the political voice of traditionally marginalized groups, i.e. women, ethnic minorities, or people from the LGBTQ community.

I recently hosted a panel-led discussion at the Arnolfini titled "Has Identity Politics Gone Too Far?" I chose this subject because many people feel that the identity politics of marginalized groups has been taken too far, and if I am completely honest, I agree to an extent. But, I also believe the identity of traditionally dominant groups have again come to the forefront of politics in recent years.

It's no myth that Donald Trump's racist and sexist language strongly appeals to people of his own identity: straight white males. Similarly, in Britain, the rhetoric from nationalist groups like UKIP and the EDL is more likely to appeal to white Brits than to non-white Brits. Of course, the same concept can apply to the whole mainstream political system; people who identify as working-class or adopt a left-wing identity have tended to vote for Labour, whereas people who identify with wealthier classes or adopt a right-wing identity have tended to vote Conservative.

In essence, there is nothing wrong with allowing your identity to influence your political views. Problems occur when you disregard and discredit the identities of others in favor of your own.

The focus at the Arnolfini event was the identity politics of marginalized groups. This was largely because many right-leaning social commentators have fervently attacked this form of identity politics, while being apparently totally oblivious to the fact that they too are asserting their identity-led perspectives. Social media has become a war zone in which any sign of caring about others is attacked as Social Justice Warrior nonsense. Conversely, when people express pride in being English, for example, it is jumped on as a sign of racism. Any sense of nuance is lost in a flurry of clacking keyboards and emojis.

The social media storm created by the recent Gillette film was a great example of this. Within hours of being published, a film raising awareness to the negative aspects of male behavior was barraged by a storm of dislikes and disgusted comments. The video sends a positive message that we all need to hear. But, generally I am very uncomfortable with the idea of a corporation riding on a social movement for profit, and doing very little else to support the cause. To others, the video undermined the identity of men and much upset was expressed in 140 characters. The video doesn't generalize all men, but maybe the negative reaction was a response to a wider issue.

Throughout history and all over the world, people in dominant groups have perpetuated destructive generalizations against those in weaker positions. Racist and sexist tropes are well known. However, people in marginalized or minority groups can certainly make sweeping generalizations about others too. Given the current backlash against identity politics, it's worth exploring this further.

Commentators from marginalized groups, such as the model Munroe Bergdorf and Labour MP Diane Abbott, are guilty of making lazy comments and leaving little space for nuance. In 2017 Bergdorf claimed that "all white people" were guilty of racial violence. Not so long ago, Abbott tweeted that "white people love playing divide and rule." While I might agree with Bergdorf and Abbott about systemic racism, such sweeping generalizations do little but antagonize and isolate people that should instead be engaged with in a firm but thoughtful way.

Statements like these just feed the trolls, adding unnecessary fuel to the fire of right-wing extremism. Bergdorf and Abbot are examples of people who have taken identity politics too far in some cases. Nonetheless, I also feel much empathy for them. When you are part of a historically marginalized group, particularly as a Black woman, it is not unusual to have strong feelings about social injustice. And sometimes that can be expressed with anger and frustration. That's OK too. But I plea that as people of color, we can find more space for nuance and allow for our passionate emotions to be used more constructively. If we are successfully able to do that, racism doesn't stand a chance.

In Bristol, the debate around the slave trader Edward Colston's legacy being plastered all over the city created a great stir. Many fear an "erasure of history" if Colston's name were to be removed from the streets of Bristol. If racist colonial men like Edward Colston, Cecil Rhodes and Winston Churchill are so precious to some people's identities, then I say keep them exactly where they are. As people who don't subscribe to this version of history, can we consider an alternative avenue for change that doesn't clash so strongly with another identity?

In any event, the colonial memorabilia provide a useful reminder that people in our nation are still proud of its history of empire, no matter what atrocities were committed. And that means we have work to do. There is no value in taking down a statue or renaming a music venue if these attitudes still permeate the culture. Our identity politics as people of color should be directed towards the education system—where we can ensure that younger generations of white Brits understand why statues of slave-traders might be offensive to their darker-skinned friends, and to all people for that matter.

Of course, the changing of surface-level iconography and conversation alone isn't enough to eradicate racism. While these things still have their value, real change will come when people organize and infiltrate or upend the very systems that perpetuate racism or inequality. The education system will not change without sustained collective action from the general public

This topic could be discussed for hours and there is undoubtedly much I have left out, including how my own identity affects my personal opinions. But there is one thing I hope readers can take away: No matter what race, class or gender you are, you are human first. Such identities can feel very real—sexism and hate crime can certainly have very tangible consequences—but we should understand identity as part of the story that we tell ourselves to help us navigate the world, and not the sole thing that defines us, or them.

By coming together and organizing with one another, we can rewrite the story and create new identities that place diversity of thought at their very foundation.

Viewpoint 3

> *"Identity politics approaches are a means for negotiating for rights in the face of discrimination. This does not apply to all identity politics approaches."*

Identity Politics Do Not Have to Be Exclusionary

Julia Ehrt

The backlash against identity politics spurred a backlash against the backlash. Included among those who believe in the value of identity politics is the author of this viewpoint, Julia Ehrt. She feels they have been misunderstood and are a necessary means to attain the rights of marginalized people, including those in the LGBTQ+ community, for which she is an advocate. However, she also argues that identity politics do not necessarily have to divide people. Dr. Julia Ehrt is executive director of the International Lesbian, Gay, Bisexual, Trans, and Intersex Association (ILGA World), an advocacy and outreach program that works closely with the United Nations to help improve LGBTQ+ rights.

"Are identity politics inevitable in order to stand up for (one's) rights?" Dr. Julia Ehrt, The Heinrich Böll Foundation, January 26, 2022, https://www.boell.de/en/2022/01/26/are-identity-politics-inevitable-in-order-to-stand-up-for-one-rights. Licensed under CC BY 4.0 International.

As you read, consider the following questions:

1. Is identity politics an essential component in the fight for equality for all people, according to this viewpoint?
2. According to this viewpoint, how do the left and the right differ in their approaches to identity politics?
3. Does the author offer any workable solutions to issues of LGBTQ+ rights?

I have been active in the LGBTQIA+ movement for over twenty years—in Germany, Europe, and the world. For our movement—or movements – that bring(s) lesbian, gay, bisexual, transgender, queer, intersex, asexual, and non-binary people together and stand(s) up for our rights, identity politics approaches seem inevitable at first.

A look at history confirms this point of view—it is full of lesbian and gay, as well as transgender, intersex, and non-binary people who have struggled against exclusion, discrimination, and violence. Identity—be it homosexual, bi, transgender, non-binary, intersex (Note: the majority of intersex people see themselves as male or female), or otherwise defined, functions as an intense, often movement-shaping experience that connects people across many different political, ideological, cultural, and geographic differences, amongst others. "Deviating from a norm" unites us.

This holds true for many groups: The clearer a group is defined and the more extreme their societal marginalization and discrimination, the stronger the bonds within that group. This has led to severe demarcation and exclusion within the LGBTQIA+ movement—many campaigns, in particular the early ones, were supported or even led by transgender people, who were then ostracized over the course of the assimilation movements of the 1980s and 1990s, especially in the Global North. As a result, the LGBTQIA+ movement continued and continues, to be dominated by gay—for the most part, white—men. Despite everything, being LGBTQIA+ is creating a tremendous, unifying moment across many social boundaries. As with any other marginalized minorities, the shared experience of structural discrimination and disenfranchisement forms the basis for group cohesion. In this context, identity politics approaches are a means for negotiating for rights in the face of discrimination. This does not apply to all identity politics approaches.

The Big Difference

Approaches towards identity politics by the right and the left differ on a fundamental level: It is indeed about access to social resources and power for both. But the Identitarian approaches of the right bolster the respective hegemon—that is, the dominant group with respect to power and resources—at the expense of all groups labelled as "different" (women, non-white, non-heterosexual people, etc.). Left-wing, progressive identity politics approaches, however, are about strengthening the societal and socio-economic participation of marginalized and disadvantaged groups. The objective here is the levelling of resources and power in terms of equality. Hence, a general critique of identity politics without specifying which kind is unproductive.

As stated at the beginning, identity politics approaches have not only proven themselves in the negotiation of equal participation for LGBTQIA+ people in Germany and elsewhere but also appear to be an opportune, legitimate, and even inevitable means in the political sphere. Ultimately, our representative democracy rests on concepts of identity, or at least on the notions of group affiliation, in that it assumes that politicians represent their voters, their constituencies, their party, and their federal state, and "get the best out of it" for those same groups—as well as to be re-elected. Even the recognition that our parliament should depict a cross-section of our society and the associated insistence that more underrepresented groups (women, BIPOC, people with a migrant background, people with a disability or disabilities, people from financially poorer families, and so on), must enter parliaments, is rooted in notions of identity or identities.

The History of Marriage Equality in the United States

Efforts to legalize same-sex marriage began to pop up across the country in the 1990s, and with it challenges on the state and national levels. Civil unions for same-sex couples existed in many states but created a separate but equal standard. At the federal level, couples were denied access to more than 1,100 federal rights and responsibilities associated with the institution, as well as those denied by their given state. The Defense of Marriage Act was signed into law in 1996 and defined marriage by the federal government as between a man and woman, thereby allowing states to deny marriage equality.

New Century & New Beginnings

As the Supreme Court decision in *Lawrence v. Texas* struck down sodomy laws in 2003, another victory was celebrated as Massachusetts became the first state to legalize same-sex marriage via a court ruling. On the federal level, however, efforts continued to prevent equality from becoming a reality. President Bush announced his opposition to same-sex marriage while the House introduced a constitutional amendment that would define marriage as between a man and a woman.

Rising Support Signals Hope

States from coast to coast began striking down past bans and enshrining marriage equality in new laws. California famously achieved marriage equality in 2008, only to have it dismantled again by the introduction and passage of Proposition 8, a ballot initiative that updated the state constitution to define marriage as between a man and a woman, that same year. The amendment later was disputed in lower level courts before making its way to the Supreme Court.

A Turning Point for Change

Only a few years after President Obama declared DOMA unconstitutional,—and instructed the Justice Department to stop defending it in court—the Supreme Court advanced marriage equality through key decisions in 2013. *Hollingsworth v. Perry* determined

Prop. 8 lacked legal standing while *United States v. Windsor* deemed DOMA unconstitutional — all but paving the way to full equality.

Marriage Equality Becomes a Reality

The moment for full marriage equality finally arrived on June 26, 2015, with the Supreme Court decision in *Obergefell v. Hodges*. In a landmark 5-4 decision, marriage equality became the law of the land and granted same-sex couples in all 50 states the right to full, equal recognition under the law.

[...]

"The Journey to Marriage Equality in the United States" by Human Rights Campaign.

Are Identity Politics Approaches Inevitable?

The flaw in or danger of identity politics approaches lies in that they easily enforce exclusion. It is also a fact that group-focused representation and organization often hampers the forging of alliances and can lead to intersectional discrimination and marginalization: If the LGBTQIA+ movement is always first about LGBTQIA+ people, this can be at the expense of the inclusion of other socially marginalized groups. Thus, women, BIPOC, people with a migrant background, and people with disabilities within the LGBTQIA+ movement are marginalized and placed at a disadvantage in that they are frequently not kept in mind when it comes to political demands. This in turn contradicts the (left) values of equal participation. It is precisely this seemingly intrinsic contradiction that left-wing identity politics is attempting to resolve, by concentrating less on identity-creating characteristics and much more on same or similar experiences. I would like to provide an example of this:

Almost fifteen years ago, I founded the Berlin-based organization TransInterQueer with other activists. Back then, we did not just want to establish an organization for transgender, intersex and queer people and advocate for their/our concerns but make a political statement beyond that. We opposed traditional identity politics in equal measure and created an organization for which the binding element was a common concern: the examination and critique of the gender binary. This made it possible for us to be an organization that was open and connected people across the narrow boundaries of trans, inter and non-binary identities—TrIQ has kept it this way to this day. If we come together and organize as people because we reject the practice of the gender binary—hetero cis women and men can also be part of the organization.

Today I work for ILGA World—the global umbrella association of LGBTQIA+ organizations with over 1,600 member organizations worldwide. And a change in mindset has also taken place at ILGA: In 2019, our general meeting adopted a new organizational strategy with an emphasis on reflecting diversity within our movement and empowering previously marginalized groups. In our language too, we are increasingly moving away from categories conceived in relation to identity politics, such as "LGBTQIA+ people" and shifting to speaking of "people with diverse sexual orientation, gender identity, gender expression and sex characteristics (SOGIESC)."

Putting the Focus on Experiences

At first glance it seems to make hardly any difference—the rewording, however, makes it clear: Every person has one or more sexual orientations, gender identities, and sex characteristics. Precisely this aspect enables us to detach our work from rigid identity categories and enter into alliances and cooperation with feminist organizations, for instance, and adjust our actions to be intersectional.

Identity is based on this perspective of mutual confirmation and recognition within a group of people with the same or similar characteristics and experiences. These commonalities can engender strong group cohesion that is ultimately based on the exclusion of others. This same exclusion is the flaw of any identity politics approach, as it ultimately contradicts left-wing values of equal participation and solidarity. Left-wing identity politics must therefore be more about foregrounding people's common concerns and not their common characteristics. If we manage to build bridges across the shared experience of mechanisms of marginalization and make that experience the foundation of political action, we will not only turn conservative identity upside down but also create a basis for political action that pushes beyond social boundaries for the good of all.

> *"Certain features of the Woke ideology, even if only on its extreme fringe, show shocking potential for being a totalitarian nightmare unfolding before our eyes."*

Wokeism Has a Breaking Point

James Lindsay

According to this viewpoint by James Lindsay, wokeism has threatened to cross the line and alienate many people who would otherwise be sympathetic to these social justice causes. He attempts to establish where this "breaking point" is in this viewpoint. He cites cancel culture involving such revered historical figures as George Washington and Abraham Lincoln to make his point and questions whether identity politics and wokeism are noble and important causes, or if they have simply gone too far and are creating moral panic. James Lindsay is an American author and mathematician.

As you read, consider the following questions:

1. Why does Lindsay consider it important to ask people where their woke breaking point is?
2. Why have historically respected presidents such as George Washington and Abraham Lincoln been the target of critical social justice in recent years?

"The Woke Breaking Point" by James Lindsay, New Discourses, June 24, 2020. Reprinted by permission.

3. What does Lindsay consider to be his woke breaking points, according to this viewpoint?

Almost everybody has a Woke Breaking Point. A point of Peak Woke. Or, at least, they should.

There should always be a line that, once crossed, signifies to someone that the ostensibly good or noble thing they currently support has soured or, as the case may be, gone completely bad. We all know the history of the twentieth century (or, so I delude myself into believing). Certain features of the Woke ideology, even if only on its extreme fringe, show shocking potential for being a totalitarian nightmare unfolding before our eyes, especially because so many good and decent people so vigorously (and viciously) support it all of a sudden. Even the rapidity with which it is spreading is disorienting, and thus alarming.

I realized the importance of establishing a "Woke breaking point" the other night while discussing the bizarre defenses of our current era with a brilliant friend. We were talking about the people in our lives who have hit their Woke breaking points and those who haven't. It struck me that many of the people in my life who remain sympathetic or outright denialist about the excesses of the Woke (Critical Social Justice) movement haven't grappled with the possibility that it isn't quite the noble and necessary cause that it sells itself to be.

What I realized is how very helpful it is for people, rather than becoming confrontational, to encourage their Woke-sympathetic friends to start identifying and naming what their non-negotiable lines will be. People's lines will—and should—vary, but as things get increasingly extreme, they will also get crossed more and more certainly. Knowing the line has been crossed, however, takes knowing there is a line and where it is.

The question to pose, then, is simple enough: What would it take for you to say that the Woke movement has gone too far?

Why should you ask this? Two reasons, given how out of hand the movement already is. First, people should be asked to grapple with the idea that things could possibly go too far, or even that they already have. Second, in circumstances like these threaten to be, everyone should stake out at least some tentative line that their current principles won't let them cross, and they need to do this before they've already crossed it and been forced to defend that which they currently find indefensible.

This simple act of getting people to commit to their principles before they let them slip is of tremendous importance and use because of how we process our moral reasoning. We do this by post-hoc rationalization, meaning that we lawyer ourselves into believing we acted morally after act, which often means after we've already crossed the line. Drawing a clear line ahead of time, especially in a social context where accountability weighs in, makes it that much easier to see the line, bright and clear, and that much harder to cross first and rationalize after.

To get real about this, you shouldn't expect this conversation to go well. It might, of course, depending on the relationship, but it's very likely to be received defensively or with an assumption that you've lost your mind. So here's some advice: Don't expect it to go well. Don't expect them to come around. Don't expect them to take you seriously. Just get the question out there where they have to think about it.

You also don't have to push the issue, and you shouldn't. If you meet resistance, it's best not to argue or damage your relationship, and you should know you won't have to. There's no need to force it. You can ask the question and then just leave them with it. The question will bother them basically forever if they refuse to play and let it. Let it do its work. It's far more important for them to grapple with than it is for you to get an answer to.

Then again, they might want to explore and engage. That's even better.

My friend and I discussed some of the breaking points that were crossed for us and for people we know. For me, it was something between seeing unfair witch-hunt-like haranguing applied to public figures I respected (falsely accusing them of racism and sexism), the subversive manipulation of language, and, especially, the brazen attacks on science coming from both the activist and scholarly communities around Critical Social Justice. This happened for me a few years ago. For my friend, it was the undeniable real racism and blatant double-standards at the heart of much of the Woke activist enterprise. For some of our friends, the public defense of riots in Woke language—like "whiteness is property," so it's okay to burn down a business—was a bridge too far. For others, it was being bullied into allyship that's never good enough. For so many more, it's just the outright racism.

Of course, I also hear from people citing the tearing down of statues (including George Washington's), people losing their jobs, people being afraid to lose their jobs, "Shut down STEM," people's relationships falling apart (including otherwise healthy interracial marriages, in particular), and a wide variety of other clear signals that things have gone too far with this moral panic and the bad ideas rising to prominence within it. For more and more people, these need to stop.

So, the question for you is: What is (or was) your Woke breaking point? The question for your friends is the same. I'd love to hear them. Post them in the comments. Where did they cross the line for you?

Even though the conversation won't go well, don't be afraid to ask about this directly, because this is important. Get specific if you need to. Ask: Whose statue has to come down? Seriously, whose is the last straw? Abraham Lincoln? Martin Luther King, Jr.? Whose? What freedom has to be stripped? Due process of law? Speech? The right not to suffer cruel and unusual punishment?

Ask: When is enough, enough? Who has to get cancelled? Fired? How many people have to lose their livelihoods? How overt does the racism have to become? How many people have to humiliate themselves in "Antiracist" Struggle Sessions? Who has to be doxxed? Destroyed? Beaten up? Killed? Does it take a public lynching? Or would it take horrors we believed we left behind in the darker chapters of the twentieth century? Where is the uncrossable line between here and there?

The questions have to be asked. They're something we have had the genuine privilege of not having to ask ourselves in a long time, and it seems like we've forgotten. Now, they have to be asked.

For one friend of mine, the line is at "real violence," whatever that means in the present era. Perhaps it's the kind the media isn't spinning excuses for, maybe it means with firearms (it seems not to include the skyrocketing violent crime rates, though). At least it's a line. At least he's thinking about it. Another, a scholar, said the obvious perversion of his own academic field would be his last straw. It's a bit fuzzy, but at least it's a line and one that seems to fall far short of violence. Violence, he even said, wouldn't be acceptable, and he's already very uneasy with the property damage and the general mayhem. At least he's thinking about it.

But, maybe it has to hit closer to home. Ask: Where is the line? Would it have to be personal? Do they have to be personally denounced a racist? Subjected to an "Antiracist" Struggle Session? Fire? Would it take destroying the thing they love? Their family? Their kids? Their job or career? Their hobby? Their life's passion? What is it? What's too far? We have to start asking, and it hardly matters if their breaking point is something selfish. People need to grapple with this. Even if all they can think about is themselves or their closest friends and family, at least they're thinking about it.

For a close friend of mine, who is quite Woke still but not at all "all in," we had to go quite far to find an absolute line. He has one. Should I, or other people he's close to and knows don't deserve it, get doxxed or start receiving credible death threats for standing up to Wokeness, that will apparently do it (does anybody deserve this, though?). Seems a little extreme to me that my own life would have to be on the line before he'd think surely this is getting out of hand, but at least he has a line. At least he's thinking about it.

The people you ask should be able to find a Woke breaking point and name it, though, and if not, they need to be pressed on that point. That's serious. They need to be asked: what does it mean that you can't imagine this going too far? Maybe it spurs no reflection. The "right side of history" is, after all, quite the Greater Good, but even this is something they need to face up to, if it's the case. Maybe that, at least, would get them thinking about it.

Again, the goal of this intervention isn't to get anyone to change their minds. It isn't even to get them to believe something horrible might be happening, is likely to happen later, or is even plausible in the current situation. It's only about getting them to engage with their principles now before the machinations of motivated reasoning lead them, eventually, to excuse what they would, as of now, see as inexcusable—at least until it happens.

VIEWPOINT 5

> *"Like pebbles dropped into a pond, the waves of conflict over wokeness ripple ever outward. But how can we maximize woke's liberating potential while minimizing divisiveness?"*

Maximizing the Potential of Identity Politics and Wokeness Without Feeding into Divisiveness

Dino Sossi

In this viewpoint, Dino Sossi discusses the lengthy history of the term "woke" as well as the current culture war surrounding it. He points out that "woke" became a more popular and expansive concept in the wake of the Black Lives Matter movement and has come to refer to numerous different progressive ideas and social justice issues. But in response to "woke" entering popular political and social discourse, it has also received backlash from those who view it as limiting free speech and disrupting the social order. Sossi argues that terms like "woke" and "identity politics" themselves create an emotional response and cause greater confusion, so avoiding easy, oversimplified labels is the best way to promote ideals central to wokeness and identity politics without feeding the flames of the culture war. Dino Sossi is an adjunct assistant professor of media studies at OCAD University in Toronto, Canada.

"How Can We Maximize Woke's Potential While Minimizing the Culture War's Divisiveness?," by Dino Sossi (OCAD University), The Conversation, March 26, 2023, https://theconversation.com/how-can-we-maximize-wokes-potential-while-minimizing-the-culture-wars-divisiveness-200989. Licensed under CC BY-ND 4.0 International.

As you read, consider the following questions:

1. When did Black Americans start using "woke" and what did it mean at that time, according to this viewpoint?
2. What is one reason the 2013 Black Lives Matter caused the definition of "woke" to broaden, according to Sossi?
3. What are some of the common criticisms of wokeness addressed in this viewpoint?

The recent collapse of Silicon Valley Bank (SVB) and other major banks has raised fears about a potential 2008-style banking crisis. While this seems unlikely, like so many events these days, SVB's failure has also been caught in the sticky rhetorical web of the culture war.

Right-wing media outlets and pundits have blamed SVB's collapse on its so-called woke practices.

In other news, Vivek Ramaswamy, author of the anti-woke book *Woke, Inc.*, recently became the latest entrant in the U.S. Republican Party's presidential primary. The entry of Vivek Ramaswamy and other potential candidates indicates that battles over wokeness will likely spill over into the next U.S. presidential election.

Old Term Meets New Movements

The term woke is not new, and its history is lengthy and tragic.

The idea was first popularized by legendary folk singer Lead Belly in his 1938 song *Scottsboro Boys*. It alludes to nine black teenagers who were falsely accused of raping two white women in Alabama in 1931. In relation to the song, Lead Belly warned, "I advise everybody, be a little careful when they go along through there—best stay woke, keep their eyes open."

Linguist Tony Thorne suggests that Black Americans started using the term in the 1940s to "mean becoming woken up or sensitized to issues of justice."

From this, wokeness initially focused on raising awareness among Black Americans of important issues impacting their community. But over time, its use expanded to encompass other social justice concerns, often in new and sometimes highly inconsistent ways.

In the wake of 2013's Black Lives Matter movement, woke's meaning quickly expanded. Part of this has to do with its social media origins. The movement subsequently became diffuse due to its unique organizational structure and social media use.

A term that was once focused on the challenges facing Black Americans within a complex political landscape expanded rapidly. Now it is used as a shorthand for a host of progressive ideas.

As a result, woke quickly became a broad rallying cry for social justice.

However, the swift spread of the term among advocates and allies was not universally welcomed. Instead, woke continued to wildly transition in opposition to the rapid expansion of social justice movements.

Waking the Anti-Woke

Right-wing politicians routinely rail against perceptions of wokeness. For example, Canadian opposition leader Pierre Poilievre has characterized himself as "anti-woke."

In 2022, former U.S. president Donald Trump criticized banks, believing they had "gone woke" and should be penalized. As such, SVB and Signature Bank are not the first banks to be caught up in the widespread hysteria over wokeness.

Congressman Matt Gaetz said that the U.S. military is too focused on wokeism. And Florida Governor Ron DeSantis has repeatedly made headlines over his government's ban on teaching certain subjects deemed woke and his rejection of corporate social advocacy.

Business executives like Ramaswamy have criticized woke capitalism and Elon Musk has recently criticized ChatGPT which he believes has gone woke.

Comedian Bill Maher frequently complains about woke's impact.

Personalities like Joe Rogan and Jordan Peterson believe it silences speech and cancels speakers.

The label woke is now frequently deployed in opposition to a variety of social movements, including fights for gender equality, climate change and LGBTQ+ rights, among others.

Like pebbles dropped into a pond, the waves of conflict over wokeness ripple ever outward. But how can we maximize woke's liberating potential while minimizing divisiveness?

Post-Woke Future

For some, the idea of being woke means to "be awake to social oppression." But for others, wokeness limits speech and threatens the prevailing order.

The result? Vicious public quarrels. We are trapped in a digital Tower of Babel built for the social media age seemingly without escape.

Open-ended terms like woke can evolve over time to symbolize more than their creators could have ever imagined. Words used ambiguously and in excess can eventually become meaningless. They can even experience semantic bleaching. This is when words lose their meaning through repeated and varied usage.

The state of play is so topsy-turvy you could argue that even anti-woke politicians can be woke. Think Poilievre advocating for drinking water for Indigenous communities. Or Trump's criminal justice reforms.

When one term is interpreted antithetically, even adopted by its avowed adversaries, it increasingly becomes meaningless.

We should resist easy labels like wokeness that simplify or disregard complex and legitimate issues. Unclear terms confuse instead of clarify, alienating those we wish to include in conversation. Society suffers and divisions harden. And marginalized individuals often suffer the most severe consequences through no fault of their own.

Periodical and Internet Sources Bibliography

The following articles have been selected to supplement the diverse views presented in this chapter.

"How Are Identity Politics Changing Democracy: An Interview with Francis Fukuyama," *The Economist*, September 14, 2018. https://www.economist.com/open-future/2018/09/14/how-are-identity-politics-changing-democracy.

Erik Edman, "Why Identity Politics Is Killing the Left," Diem25, January 18, 2021. https://diem25.org/the-uselessness-empty-symbols/.

Michelle I. Gao, "Why I Don't Support Identity Politics Anymore," *The Harvard Crimson*, January 24, 2018. https://www.thecrimson.com/article/2018/1/24/gao-identity-politics/.

Kenneth J. Gergen, "Social Construction and the Transformation of Identity Politics," Swarthmore College, 1999. https://www.swarthmore.edu/sites/default/files/assets/documents/kenneth-gergen/Social%20Construction_and_the_Transformation.pdf.

James Livingston, "Two Cheers for Identity Politics," Project Syndicate, June 21, 2024. https://www.project-syndicate.org/commentary/explaining-and-defending-identity-politics-by-james-livingston-2024-06.

Joan D. Mandle, "How Political is the Personal?: Identity Politics, Feminism and Social Change," WMST-L. https://userpages.umbc.edu/~korenman/wmst/identity_pol.html

Alan Martin, "The Psychology of Changing Political Viewpoints," Wired, October 4, 2013. https://www.wired.com/story/changing-political-beliefs.

Rachel Murray, "Rethinking Divisiveness: Identity Politics and the Real Issues We Face," Inclusion Geeks, April 30, 2024. https://www.shegeeksout.com/articles/rethinking-divisiveness-identity-politics-and-the-real-issues-we-face/.

Nancy Whittier, "Identity Politics, Consciousness Raising and, Visibility Politics," Smith College. https://www.smith.edu/sites/default/files/media/Faculty/Identity%20Politics,%20Consciousness%20Raising,%20and%20Visibility%20Politics%20Oxford%20Handbook%20%20postprint.pdf.

George Yancey, "Identity Politics, Political Ideology and Well-Being: Is Identity Politics Good for Our Well-Being?" *Sociological Forum,* October 12, 2023. https://onlinelibrary.wiley.com/doi/10.1111/socf.12966.

OPPOSING VIEWPOINTS® SERIES

Chapter 4

How Much Do Identity Politics Contribute to Political and Social Polarization?

Chapter Preface

Has identity politics worked at creating positive change? Has it had the opposite effect, causing nothing but polarization and division? The answer likely lies somewhere in between. That identity politics has increased awareness of the struggles and injustices faced by marginalized people, such as those in the LGBTQ+ community and racial minorities, is undeniable. That it has sown anger and resentment among many people, particularly across partisan lines, is equally indisputable.

The latter trend seemed inevitable. Any push in favor of groups of people is destined to be followed by a pushback from others against it, whether due to a desire to maintain the status quo or resentment that their struggles are being ignored or minimized. It has been claimed that the battles that resulted in an embracing of identity politics and wokeism have been and will be worth the fight. But it has also been asserted that it has not only alienated a wide swath of Americans and others around the world, but has divided Democrats and progressives into separate camps and pushed some voters to the Republican base.

This chapter features a variety of opinions about the effectiveness of identity politics. Some argue that identity politics will soon come to an end in the wake of the increased polarization it has caused in American society. Others assert that it has helped further the cause of equal rights for marginalized communities and raised awareness of the injustices they have faced and continue to face.

The first viewpoint in this chapter addresses a logical consequence of identity politics, which is that it has increased interest in political and social issues. The proof is at the polls in the United States, where turnout has increased dramatically in both midterm and presidential election cycles, particularly since Donald Trump, easily the most controversial and polarizing America political figure of the 21st century, announced his candidacy in 2015 and won the presidency a year later.

Is identity politics beneficial to politicians on the left who support it, or on the right who oppose it? It has been claimed that moderates have been trampled in recent years by extremists on both sides who either embrace or reject wokeism and cancel culture. Is identity politics relevant in the lives of ordinary people? This chapter will delve deeply into all these questions.

Viewpoint 1

> *"Race and ethnicity are fundamental dividing lines in American politics, with political preferences and electoral participation varying greatly by race and ethnicity."*

Has Identity Politics Increased Voter Turnout?

Hannah Hartig, Andrew Daniller, Scott Keeter, and Ted Van Green

This viewpoint from the Pew Research Center explains how identity politics has played a role in the polarization of voters while also helping increase turnout at the polls. Different social identities based on race, ethnicity, education, and age reveal different patterns in voting, suggesting that one's social identity plays an important role in how one votes, and an increased sense of division between different groups has resulted in greater political engagement. Hannah Hartig is a senior researcher at Pew Research Center, where Andrew Daniller is a research associate, Scott Keeter is a senior survey advisor, and Ted Van Green is a research analyst.

As you read, consider the following questions:

1. How did voter turnout for the 2020 presidential election compare to previous presidential elections?

"Voter turnout" by Hannah Hartig, Andrew Daniller, Scott Keeter, and Ted Van Green, Pew Research Center, July 12, 2023.

2. What political party do Black voters favor, according to data cited in this viewpoint?
3. What percent of voters were adults over 50 in the 2022 midterm election?

The elections of 2018, 2020 and 2022 were three of the highest-turnout U.S. elections of their respective types in decades. About two-thirds (66%) of the voting-eligible population turned out for the 2020 presidential election—the highest rate for any national election since 1900. The 2018 election (49% turnout) had the highest rate for a midterm since 1914. Even the 2022 election's turnout, with a slightly lower rate of 46%, exceeded that of all midterm elections since 1970.

While sizable shares of the public vote either consistently or not at all, many people vote intermittently. Given how closely divided the U.S. is politically, these intermittent voters often determine the outcome of elections and how the balance of support for the two major political parties swings between elections.

Overall, 70% of U.S. adult citizens who were eligible to participate in all three elections between 2018 and 2022 voted in at least one of them, with about half that share (37%) voting in all three.

Adults who voted in at least one election during the period divide evenly between Democrats and independents who lean toward the Democratic Party or Republicans and Republican-leaning independents in their current party affiliation (48% each). The subset who voted in all three elections are similarly divided (49% Democrats, 50% Republicans). Citizens who did not vote in any of the three tilt Republican by 46% to 41%.

Democrats outnumbered Republicans among the 8% of adult citizens who voted in 2018 and 2020 but not 2022 (55% Democratic, 40% Republican). A similar-sized group

(8%) voted in 2020 and 2022 but not 2018, and this group's composition tilts Republican (57%, vs. 40% Democratic). The 12% who voted in 2020 and opted out of both the 2018 and 2022 midterms were roughly evenly divided among Democrats (46%) and Republicans (43%).

Given the sizable number of intermittent voters and chronic nonvoters, as well as the fact that this group, collectively, is fairly evenly divided in partisan affiliation, both parties have plenty of potential supporters on the sidelines in any given election.

Political Preferences Differ A Lot by Race and Ethnicity . . . and So Does Voter Turnout

Race and ethnicity are fundamental dividing lines in American politics, with political preferences and electoral participation varying greatly by race and ethnicity. In the current partisan alignment, Black, Hispanic and Asian voters are all majority Democratic groups, to different degrees, though Republican candidates have gained some ground in the past four years among Hispanic voters.

Black voters remain Democratic stalwarts, voting 93% to 5% for the party's candidates for U.S. House in 2022. Hispanic and Asian voters clearly favored Democratic candidates as well, but by narrower margins: 60% to 39% for Hispanic voters, and 68% to 32% for Asian voters.

But White Americans are much more consistent voters than Black, Hispanic or Asian Americans. Compared with the national average of 37% who voted in 2018, 2020 and 2022, 43% of White citizens who were age eligible to vote in all three elections did so; just 24% did not vote in any of these.

Black, Hispanic and Asian adults lagged far behind, with 27% of Black, 19% of Hispanic and 21% of Asian age-eligible citizens voting in all three elections. Hispanic citizens were most likely to have not voted in any of the most recent three general elections (47%, compared with 36% for Black and 31% for Asian citizens ages 22 and older in 2022).

Differences by Education

Over the past few election cycles, Republicans have gained ground among White adults who do not have a college degree, who make up 41% of eligible voters. This group is about average in its consistency of voter turnout, with 35% of those ages 22 and over in 2022 voting in 2018, 2020 and 2022, and 31% voting in none of these three elections. White voters without a college degree favored Republican House candidates 66% to 32% in 2022.

By contrast, White adults with college degrees vote at very high rates: 56% of those eligible turned out in all three elections and just 13% participated in none of them. College-educated White adults make up 24% of the eligible electorate but about a third of voters in 2022 (34%). White voters with college degrees had tilted Republican for several decades, but in the past four elections have favored Democratic candidates (52% to 47% in 2022).

The education gap in White voters' preferences in 2022 was not apparent among either Black or Hispanic voters (the sample size of Asian voters without a college degree was too small to produce a reliable estimate). College-educated Black and Hispanic adults also voted at higher rates than Black and Hispanic adults without a college degree in each of the three elections.

A small education gap appeared in 2020 presidential preference among Hispanic voters: College-educated Hispanic voters preferred Biden by a margin of 69% to 29%, while Hispanic voters without a college degree preferred Biden by a somewhat narrower margin (58% to 39%). But no significant education gap in candidate preference was observed for Black or Hispanic voters in 2018 or 2022, nor for Black voters in 2020.

The upshot of racial differences in candidate preference and turnout patterns is that Republican candidates benefited from both the relatively large size of the White adult population without a college degree and their somewhat higher turnout rates compared with Black, Hispanic and Asian adults.

Growth in support for Democratic candidates among White voters with a college degree, along with the high turnout levels among this group, offset some of the growth in support for the Republican Party among White voters without a college degree. But college-educated White adults remain a smaller share of all eligible voters than White adults without a college degree.

Voters and Nonvoters

The two most recent midterms—2022 and 2018—both featured unusually high turnout compared with nearly every other recent midterm election year. But the differences between those who turned out to vote in 2022 versus 2018—and between those who did not vote—accounted for much of the difference in outcomes between the two elections.

The stark demographic differences between voters and nonvoters in 2022 are similar to those seen in previous U.S. elections.

Voters were much older, on average, than nonvoters. Adults under 50 made up 36% of voters, but 64% of nonvoters. This is very similar to the pattern seen in 2018—although those under 50 made up a somewhat larger share of voters in 2018 (40%).

Turnout also differed by race and ethnicity.

Three-quarters of voters (75%) were White, non-Hispanic adults. But this group accounted for a smaller share (55%) of nonvoters. Hispanic adults and Black, non-Hispanic adults each made up 9% of voters, but slightly larger shares of nonvoters (18% and 15%, respectively). Asian Americans made up 3% of voters, and a slightly higher share (5%) of nonvoters. These differences are nearly identical to the patterns seen in 2018.

There are also large educational and income differences between voters and nonvoters. Adults with a college degree made up 43% of voters in 2022, but only 25% of nonvoters. Those without a college degree made up 56% of voters, but 74% of nonvoters.

Voting Methods in the 2022 Election

As concerns over the COVID-19 pandemic declined, fewer voters reported having voted absentee or by mail in 2022 than in 2020.

In 2022, 43% of voters said they cast their ballot in person on Election Day. A somewhat smaller share (36%) said they cast an absentee or mail-in ballot, and 21% said they voted in person before Election Day.

In the 2020 election, held during the first year of the coronavirus pandemic, 45% of voters said they cast their ballots by absentee or mail-in ballot, while identical shares (27%) said they voted in person either on Election Day or beforehand.

As was the case in 2020, voters who supported Republican candidates were more likely to report having voted in person on Election Day than by other methods. About half (51%) of those who supported Republicans said they voted this way, while smaller shares said they voted by mail or absentee ballot (27%) or voted in person before Election Day (22%). In 2020, 38% said they voted in person on Election Day, while somewhat smaller shares said they voted by mail or absentee (32%) or voted in person before Election Day (30%).

Voters who supported Democratic candidates were more likely to say they cast absentee or mail-in ballots (45%). About one-third (34%) said they voted in person on Election Day and two-in-ten said they voted in person before Election Day. In 2020, a 58% majority said they voted by mail or absentee ballot, while just 17% said they voted in person on Election Day.

Reflecting these patterns, Republicans won a majority of votes among those who said they voted in person on Election

Day, 60% to 38%. Democrats won—by an identical margin—voters who said they voted by mail or absentee ballot. Those who said they voted in person before Election Day were divided: 53% supported Republican candidates, while 46% voted for Democratic candidates.

Viewpoint 2

> *"Drawing from this lore, contemporary gun culture romanticizes the 'good guy with a gun' as the patriotic protector of the peace and a bulwark against government overreach."*

The Right Uses Identity Politics for Votes, Too

Ryan Neville-Shepard and Casey Ryan Kelly

As this viewpoint by Ryan Neville-Shepard and Casey Ryan Kelly indicates, the left isn't the only side of the political divide to use identity politics. With increasing polarization, more white conservative voters have felt that their values and lifestyles are under attack. Candidates have made use of these white identity politics by promising to protect this social group from marginalization. The authors cite the frequent use of guns in campaign ads as evidence that conservatives are appealing to white racial solidarity, as guns have symbolically been linked to protecting the interests of white people since early in U.S. history. By appealing to white voters to help protect the conservative way of life, conservative candidates and politicians are also appealing to identity politics. Ryan Neville-Shepard is an associate professor of communication at the University of Arkansas and Casey Ryan Kelly is a professor of communication studies at the University of Nebraska, Lincoln.

"Militant White Identity Politics on Full Display in GOP Political Ads Featuring High-Powered Weapons," by Ryan Neville-Shepard (University of Arkansas) and Casey Ryan Kelly (University of Nebraska, Lincoln), The Conversation, July 11, 2022, https://theconversation.com/militant-white-identity-politics-on-full-display-in-gop-political-ads-featuring-high-powered-weapons-185671. Licensed under CC BY-ND 4.0 International.

As you read, consider the following questions:

1. What examples do the authors cite of guns being linked to defending the interests of white people?
2. How do contemporary gun laws reflect the connection between guns and whiteness?
3. What do candidates suggest they are protecting white conservative voters from?

Republican Eric Greitens, a candidate for Missouri's open U.S. Senate seat, shocked viewers with a new online political ad in June 2022 that encouraged his supporters to go "RINO hunting."

Appearing with a shotgun and a smirk, Greitens leads the hunt for RINOs, shorthand for the derisive "Republicans In Name Only." Along with armed soldiers, Greitens is storming a house under the cover of a smoke grenade.

"Join the MAGA crew," Greitens says in the video. "Get a RINO hunting permit. There's no bagging limit, no tagging limit and it doesn't expire until we save our country."

The ad comes from a candidate who has repeatedly found himself in controversy, having resigned as Missouri's governor amid accusations of sexual assault and allegations of improper campaign financing that sparked an 18-month investigation that eventually cleared him of any legal wrongdoing.

The political ad was also launched—and quickly removed—from Facebook and flagged by Twitter at a time when the nation is still coming to terms with the insurrection at the U.S. Capitol and reeling from mass shootings in Tulsa, Oklahoma, Uvalde, Texas, Buffalo, New York and Highland Park, Illinois.

The ad continues to circulate on YouTube via various news sources.

Greitens's call to political arms is hardly new.

In his 2016 gubernatorial ads, Greitens appeared firing a Gatling-style machine gun into the air and using an M4 rifle to create an explosion in a field to demonstrate his resistance to the Obama administration.

What Greitens' ad represents, in our view, is the evolution of the use of guns in political ads as a coded appeal for white voters.

While they might have been a bit more ambiguous in the past, candidates are increasingly making these appeals appear more militant in their culture war against ideas and politicians they oppose.

Guns as a Symbol of Whiteness

As communication scholars, we have studied the ways that white masculinity has influenced contemporary conservative populism.

We have also examined the ways that racial appeals to white voters have evolved under the GOP's Southern strategy, the long game that conservatives have played since the 1960s to weaken the Democratic Party in the South by exploiting racial animus.

In some of our latest work, we have examined the ways that guns have been used in campaign ads to represent white identity politics, or what political scientist Ashley Jardina has explained as the way that white racial solidarity and fears of marginalization have manifested in a political movement.

Symbolically, guns in the U.S. have historically been linked to defending the interests of white people.

In her book *Loaded: A Disarming History of the Second Amendment*, historian Roxanne Dunbar-Ortiz documents how America's Founding Fathers originally conceived of the Second Amendment as protection for white frontier militias in their efforts to subdue and exterminate Indigenous people. The Second Amendment was also designed to safeguard Southern slave owners who feared revolts.

As a result, the right to bear arms was never imagined by the founders to be an individual liberty held by Indigenous people and people of color.

As illustrated in Richard Slotkin's book *Gunfighter Nation: The Myth of the Frontier in Twentieth-Century America*, the popular film and literary genre of the Western glamorized white, hypermasculine cowboys and gunslingers "civilizing" the wild frontier to make it safe for white homesteaders.

Drawing from this lore, contemporary gun culture romanticizes the "good guy with a gun" as the patriotic protector of the peace and a bulwark against government overreach.

Contemporary gun laws reflect a historic racial disparity concerning who is authorized and under what circumstances individuals are allowed to use lethal force.

For example, so-called "stand your ground" laws have been used historically to justify the killing of Black men, most notably in the Trayvon Martin case.

Gun control advocates Everytown for Gun Safety have found that homicides resulting from white shooters killing Black victims are "deemed justifiable five times more frequently than when the shooter is Black and the victim is white."

Militant White Identity Politics

Featuring a gun in a political ad has become an easy way to get attention, but our research has found that its meaning has shifted in recent years.

In a 2010 race for Alabama agriculture commissioner, Dale Peterson was featured in an ad holding a gun, wearing a cowboy hat and talking in a deep Southern drawl about the need to challenge the "thugs and criminals" in government.

His style proved entertaining.

Though Peterson placed third in his race, political analysts like *Time* magazine's Dan Fletcher raved that he created one of the best campaign ads ever.

In the same year, Arizona Republican Pam Gorman ran for U.S. Congress.

She took the use of guns in political ads even further by appearing at a backyard range and firing a machine gun, pistol, AR-15 and a revolver in the same ad.

Though she gained attention for her provocative tactics, Gorman eventually lost to Ben Quayle, son of former Vice President Dan Quayle, in a 10-candidate primary.

Aside from the shock value, guns in ads became a symbol of opposition to the Obama administration.

For instance, in 2014, U.S. congressional candidate Will Brooke of Alabama ran an online ad in a Republican primary showing him loading a copy of the Obamacare legislation into a truck, driving it into the woods and shooting it with a handgun, rifle and assault rifle.

Not done, the remains of the copy were then thrown into a wood chipper. Although Brooke lost the seven-way primary, his ad received national attention.

The call to defend a conservative way of life got increasingly bizarre—and became a common tactic for GOP candidates.

Well before Greitens, U.S. congressional candidate Kay Daly from North Carolina fired a shotgun at the end of an ad during her unsuccessful campaign in 2015 asking supporters to join her in hunting RINOs.

The ad attacked her primary opponent, incumbent Rep. Renee Elmers, a Republican from North Carolina, for funding Obamacare, "Planned Butcherhood" and protecting rights of "illegal alien child molesters."

Before he drew the ire of Trump, Brian Kemp climbed the polls in Georgia's race for governor in 2018 with an ad titled "Jake" in which he interviewed his daughter's boyfriend.

Holding a shotgun in his lap as he sat in a chair, Kemp portrayed himself as a conservative outsider ready to take a "chainsaw to government regulations" and demanding respect as his family's patriarch.

The ads of the most recent cycle build on this development of the gun as a symbol of white resistance.

Conservative GOP Rep. Marjorie Taylor Greene, from Georgia, ran an ad for a gun giveaway in 2021 that she made in response to what she claimed was Biden's arming of Islamic terrorists as well as

Speaker of the House Nancy Pelosi's allegedly sneaking the Green New Deal and other liberal legislation into a budget proposal.

Firing a weapon from a truck, she announced she would "blow away the Democrats' socialist agenda."

The Culture Wars Continue

Surrounding himself with soldiers, Greitens goes further than those before him in this latest iteration of the Republican use of guns.

But his strategy is not out of the ordinary for a party that has increasingly relied on provocative images of violent resistance to speak to white voters.

Despite the violence of Jan. 6, conservatives are still digging their own trenches.

VIEWPOINT 3

> *"When building tribal boundaries between 'us' and 'them,' some politicians have managed very well to create virtual groups of people that do not communicate and hate without even knowing each other: This is the human animal in action!"*

Tribalism Contributes to Political Division and Violence

Arash Javanbakht

In this viewpoint, Arash Javanbakht explains how politicians use fear to encourage tribalism and political division. The fear of "the others"—or people who are different from ourselves—has frequently been mobilized recently to encourage voters to support one political party or the other. Fear and the tribalism it encourages make people trust others who are like them—meaning those who share a social identity—and distrust people who aren't. It causes people to act illogically and disregard available information, and at its most severe it can lead to acts of violence, including political violence. Arash Javanbakht is an assistant professor of psychiatry at Wayne State University in Detroit, Michigan.

"The Politics of Fear: How It Manipulates Us to Tribalism," by Arash Javanbakht (Wayne State University), The Conversation, March 19, 2019, https://theconversation.com/the-politics-of-fear-how-it-manipulates-us-to-tribalism-113815. Licensed under CC BY-ND 4.0 International.

As you read, consider the following questions:

1. What example does Javanbakht provide of former President Trump appealing to fear and tribalism?
2. According to the author, how long has tribalism been a part of human behavior?
3. What historic examples of harmful tribalism does Javanbakht cite?

People have always used fear for intimidation of the subordinates or enemies, and shepherding the tribe by the leaders. Recently, it appears that Pres. Trump has used fear by suggesting in a tweet that four minority congresswomen go back to the places they came from.

There is a longstanding history of employing the fear of "the others," turning humans into illogical ruthless weapons, in service to an ideology. Fear is a very strong tool that can blur humans' logic and change their behavior.

Fear is arguably as old as life. It is deeply ingrained in the living organisms that have survived extinction through billions of years of evolution. Its roots are deep in our core psychological and biological being, and it is one of our most intimate feelings. Danger and war are as old as human history, and so are politics and religion.

I am a psychiatrist and neuroscientist specializing in fear and trauma, and I have some evidence-based thoughts on how fear is abused in politics.

We Learn Fear from Tribe Mates

Like other animals, we humans can learn fear from experience, such as being attacked by a predator. We also learn from observation, such as witnessing a predator attacking another human. And, we learn by instructions, such as being told there is a predator nearby.

Learning from our conspecifics—members of the same species—is an evolutionary advantage that has prevented us from repeating dangerous experiences of other humans. We have a tendency to trust our tribe mates and authorities, especially when it comes to danger. It is adaptive: Parents and wise old men told us not to eat a special plant, or not to go to an area in the woods, or we would be hurt. By trusting them, we would not die like a great-grandfather who died eating that plant. This way we accumulated knowledge.

Tribalism has been an inherent part of the human history. There has always been competition between groups of humans in different ways and with different faces, from brutal wartime nationalism to a strong loyalty to a football team. Evidence from cultural neuroscience shows that our brains even respond differently at an unconscious level simply to the view of faces from other races or cultures.

At a tribal level, people are more emotional and consequently less logical: Fans of both teams pray for their team to win, hoping God will take sides in a game. On the other hand, we regress to tribalism when afraid. This is an evolutionary advantage that would lead to the group cohesion and help us fight the other tribes to survive.

Tribalism is the biological loophole that many politicians have banked on for a long time: tapping into our fears and tribal instincts. Some examples are Nazism, the Ku Klux Klan, religious wars and the Dark Ages. The typical pattern is to give the other humans a different label than us, and say they are going to harm us or our resources, and to turn the other group into a concept. It does not have to necessarily be race or nationality, which are used very often. It can be any real or imaginary difference: liberals, conservatives, Middle Easterners, white men, the right, the left, Muslims, Jews, Christians, Sikhs. The list goes on and on.

When building tribal boundaries between "us" and "them," some politicians have managed very well to create virtual groups of people that do not communicate and hate without even knowing each other: This is the human animal in action!

Fear Is Uninformed

A soldier once told me: "It is much easier to kill someone you have never met, from distance. When you look through the scope, you just see a red dot, not a human." The less you know about them, the easier to fear them, and to hate them.

This human tendency and ability of destruction of what is unknown and unfamiliar is meat to the politicians who want to exploit fear: If you grew up only around people who look like you, only listened to one media outlet and heard from the old uncle that those who look or think differently hate you and are dangerous, the inherent fear and hatred toward those unseen people is an understandable (but flawed) result.

To win us, politicians, sometimes with the media's help, do their best to keep us separated, to keep the real or imaginary "others" just a "concept." Because if we spend time with others, talk to them and eat with them, we will learn that they are like us: humans with all the strengths and weaknesses that we possess. Some are strong, some are weak, some are funny, some are dumb, some are nice and some not too nice.

Fear Is Illogical and Often Dumb

Very often my patients with phobias start with: "I know it is stupid, but I am afraid of spiders." Or it may be dogs or cats, or something else. And I always reply: "It is not stupid, it is illogical." We humans have different functions in the brain, and fear oftentimes bypasses logic. There are several reasons. One is that logic is slow; fear is fast. In situations of danger, we ought to be fast: First run or kill, then think.

Politicians and the media very often use fear to circumvent our logic. I always say the U.S. media are disaster pornographers—they work too much on triggering their audiences' emotions. They are kind of political reality shows, surprising to many from outside the U.S.

When one person kills a few others in a city of millions, which is of course a tragedy, major networks' coverage could lead one to perceive the whole city is under siege and unsafe. If one undocumented illegal immigrant murders a U.S. citizen, some politicians use fear with the hope that few will ask: "This is terrible, but how many people were murdered in this country by U.S. citizens just today?" Or: "I know several murders happen every week in this town, but why am I so scared now that this one is being showcased by the media?"

We do not ask these questions, because fear bypasses logic.

Fear Can Turn Violent

There is a reason that the response to fear is called the "fight or flight" response. That response has helped us survive the predators and other tribes that have wanted to kill us. But again, it is another loophole in our biology to be abused to turn on our aggression toward "the others," whether in the form of vandalizing their temples or harassing them on the social media.

When ideologies manage to get hold of our fear circuitry, we often regress to illogical, tribal and aggressive human animals, becoming weapons ourselves—weapons that politicians use for their own agenda.

Viewpoint 4

> *"Those who voted in 2018 but not in 2016 backed Biden over Trump in the 2020 election by about two-to-one."*

How Identity Impacts Presidential Elections

Ruth Igielnik, Scott Keeter, and Hannah Hartig

This viewpoint from the Pew Research Center digs deeply into the reasons Joe Biden beat Donald Trump in the 2020 presidential election by looking at the demographics of voters and examining the role that various types of social identity played in this outcome. Huge voter turnout certainly helped shape this election, but support from certain demographic groups proved most essential. Appealing to social identity groups and encouraging them to vote can have a major impact on elections. Ruth Igielnik is a former senior researcher at Pew Research Center, where Scott Keeter is a senior survey advisor and Hannah Hartig is a senior researcher.

As you read, consider the following questions:

1. What were the differences between voters Trump brought into the 2020 election and voters Biden brought in?
2. How did gender factor into how people voted in the 2020 presidential election?

"Behind Biden's 2020 Victory" by Ruth Igielnik, Scott Keeter, and Hannah Hartig, Pew Research Center, June 30, 2021.

3. How did geographic divisions impact the 2020 election and other recent elections?

The 2020 presidential election was historic in many ways. Amid a global pandemic, with unprecedented changes in how Americans voted, voter turnout rose 7 percentage points over 2016, resulting in a total of 66% of U.S. adult citizens casting a ballot in the 2020 election. Joe Biden defeated Donald Trump 306-232 in the Electoral College and had a 4-point margin in the popular vote. While Biden's popular vote differential was an improvement over Hillary Clinton's 2016 2-point advantage, it was not as resounding as congressional Democrats' 9-point advantage over Republicans in votes cast in the 2018 elections for the U.S. House of Representatives.

A new analysis of validated 2020 voters from Pew Research Center's American Trends Panel examines change and continuity in the electorate, both of which contributed to Biden's victory. It looks at how new voters and voters who turned out in one or both previous elections voted in the 2020 presidential election and offers a detailed portrait of the demographic composition and vote choices of the 2020 electorate. It also provides a comparison with findings from our previous studies of the 2016 and 2018 electorates.

A number of factors determined the composition of the 2020 electorate and explain how it delivered Biden a victory. Among those who voted for Clinton and Trump in 2016, similar shares of each—about nine-in-ten—also turned out in 2020, and the vast majority remained loyal to the same party in the 2020 presidential contest. These voters formed substantial bases of support for both Biden and Trump. Overall, there were shifts in presidential candidate support among some key groups between 2016 and 2020, notably suburban voters and independents. On balance, these shifts helped Biden a little more than Trump.

Validated Voters, Defined

Members of Pew Research Center's nationally representative American Trends Panel were matched to public voting records from three national commercial voter files in an attempt to find a record for voting in the 2020 election. Validated voters are citizens who told us in a post-election survey that they voted in the 2020 general election and have a record for voting in a commercial voter file. Nonvoters are citizens who were not found to have a record of voting in any of the voter files or told us they did not vote.

Overall, one-in-four 2020 voters (25%) had not voted in 2016. About a quarter of these (6% of all 2020 voters) showed up two years later—in 2018—to cast ballots in the highest-turnout midterm election in decades. Those who voted in 2018 but not in 2016 backed Biden over Trump in the 2020 election by about two-to-one (62% to 36%).

Both Trump and Biden were able to bring new voters into the political process in 2020. The 19% of 2020 voters who did not vote in 2016 or 2018 split roughly evenly between the two candidates (49% Biden vs. 47% Trump). However, as with voters overall, there was a substantial age divide within this group. Among those under age 30 who voted in 2020 but not in either of the two previous elections, Biden led 59% to 33%, while Trump won among new or irregular voters ages 30 and older by 55% to 42%. Younger voters also made up an outsize share of these voters: Those under age 30 made up 38% of new or irregular 2020 voters, though they represented just 15% of all 2020 voters.

One somewhat unusual aspect of the 2016 election was the relatively high share of voters (nearly 6%) who voted for one of the third-party candidates (mostly the Libertarian and Green Party nominees), a fact many observers attributed to the relative unpopularity of both major party candidates. By comparison, just 2% of voters chose a third-party candidate in 2020. Overall, third-party 2016 voters who turned out in

2020 voted 53%-36% for Biden over Trump, with 10% opting for a third-party candidate. Among the 5% of Republicans who voted third-party in 2016 and voted in 2020, a majority (70%) supported Trump in 2020, but 18% backed Biden. Among the 5% of Democrats who voted third-party in 2016 and voted in 2020, just 8% supported Trump in 2020 while 85% voted for Biden.

Here are some of the other key findings from the analysis:

- Biden made gains with suburban voters. In 2020, Biden improved upon Clinton's vote share with suburban voters: 45% supported Clinton in 2016 vs. 54% for Biden in 2020. This shift was also seen among White voters: Trump narrowly won White suburban voters by 4 points in 2020 (51%-47%); he carried this group by 16 points in 2016 (54%-38%). At the same time, Trump grew his vote share among rural voters. In 2016, Trump won 59% of rural voters, a number that rose to 65% in 2020.
- Trump made gains among Hispanic voters. Even as Biden held on to a majority of Hispanic voters in 2020, Trump made gains among this group overall. There was a wide educational divide among Hispanic voters: Trump did substantially better with those without a college degree than college-educated Hispanic voters (41% vs. 30%).
- Apart from the small shift among Hispanic voters, Joe Biden's electoral coalition looked much like Hillary Clinton's, with Black, Hispanic and Asian voters and those of other races casting about four-in-ten of his votes. Black voters remained overwhelmingly loyal to the Democratic Party, voting 92%-8% for Biden.
- Biden made gains with men, while Trump improved among women, narrowing the gender gap. The gender gap in the 2020 election was narrower than it had been in 2016, both because of gains that Biden made among men and because of gains Trump made among women. In 2020, men were almost evenly divided between Trump and Biden, unlike in 2016 when Trump won men by 11 points. Trump won

a slightly larger share of women's votes in 2020 than in 2016 (44% vs. 39%), while Biden's share among women was nearly identical to Clinton's (55% vs. 54%).

- Biden improved over Clinton among White non-college voters. White voters without a college degree were critical to Trump's victory in 2016, when he won the group by 64% to 28%. In 2018, Democrats were able to gain some ground with these voters, earning 36% of the White, non-college vote to Republicans' 61%. In 2020, Biden roughly maintained Democrats' 2018 share among the group, improving upon Clinton's 2016 performance by receiving the votes of 33%. But Trump's share of the vote among this group—who represented 42% of the total electorate this year—was nearly identical to his vote share in 2016 (65%).
- Biden grew his support with some religious groups while Trump held his ground. Both Trump and Biden held onto or gained with large groups within their respective religious coalitions. Trump's strong support among White evangelical Protestants ticked up (77% in 2016, 84% in 2020) while Biden got more support among atheists and agnostics than did Clinton in 2016.
- After decades of constituting the majority of voters, Baby Boomers and members of the Silent Generation made up less than half of the electorate in 2020 (44%), falling below the 52% they constituted in both 2016 and 2018. Gen Z and Millennial voters favored Biden over Trump by margins of about 20 points, while Gen Xers and Boomers were more evenly split in their preferences. Gen Z voters, those ages 23 and younger, constituted 8% of the electorate, while Millennials and Gen Xers made up 47% of 2020 voters.
- A record number of voters reported casting ballots by mail in 2020—including many voters who said it was their first time doing so. Nearly half of 2020 voters (46%) said they had voted by mail or absentee, and among that group, about four-in-ten said it was their first time casting a ballot

> this way. Hispanic and White voters were more likely than Black voters to have cast absentee or mail ballots, while Black voters were more likely than White or Hispanic voters to have voted early in person. Urban and suburban voters were also more likely than rural voters to have voted absentee or by mail ballot.

This analysis is based on a survey of 11,818 members of Pew Research Center's American Trends Panel conducted Nov. 12-17, 2020, shortly after the general election. It also draws on surveys conducted among 10,640 panelists from Nov. 7-16, 2018, after the midterm election that year and 4,183 panelists from Nov. 29 to Dec. 12, 2016, after the general election. Researchers attempted to match the panelists to three different commercial voter files that contain official records of voter registration and turnout for 2016, 2018 and 2020.

This study marries official turnout records with a post-election survey among a large, ongoing survey panel, with the goal of improving the accuracy of the results compared with relying on self-reported turnout alone. The survey panel also makes it possible to examine change in turnout and vote preference over time among many of the same individuals. This analysis joins a growing body of research seeking to achieve a more accurate assessment of the 2020 election, each based on somewhat different sources of data.Different methods and data sources have unique strengths and weaknesses, meaning that specific estimates are likely to vary among the studies and no single resource can be considered definitive.

Voting Patterns in the 2020 Election

The 2020 election featured continuity in the voting patterns of major demographic and political groups in the population, but there were a few important shifts. The gender gap in the 2020 election was narrower than it had been in 2016 as Democrats made gains among men and Republicans made gains among women. In the 2016 election, Donald Trump won men by 11 percentage points (52% to 41%) while Hillary Clinton won women by 15 points (54% to 39%). In the 2018 election, Democrats substantially narrowed the gap with men (50% of men voted for Democratic candidates, 48% for Republican candidates) while maintaining an 18-point lead among women. In the 2020 election, men again divided nearly evenly (50% Trump, 48% Biden), while Biden's advantage narrowed to 11 points among women (55% to 44%).

Similarly, as Biden increased his level of support among White men in the 2020 election relative to Clinton's in 2016, Trump gained among White women, which had the effect of further narrowing the gender gap among White voters. In 2016, Trump won White men by 30 points (62% to 32%). That gap narrowed to a 17-point margin for Trump in 2020 (57% to 40%). White women, a group sometimes categorized as swing voters and who broke nearly evenly in 2016 (47% for Trump to 45% for Clinton), favored him in 2020 (53% to 46%).

Biden received the support of 92% of Black voters, nearly the same as Clinton received in 2016 and Democratic candidates for the U.S. House received in 2018.

While Biden took a 59% majority of the Hispanic vote, Trump (with 38%) gained significantly over the level of support Republican candidates for the House received in 2018 (25%). To be sure, Hispanic voters are not a monolith; there is substantial diversity within the Hispanic electorate.

One noteworthy feature of the 2020 election was the wide education gap among Hispanic voters. In 2020, Biden won college-educated Hispanic voters 69% to 30%. At the same time, Biden's advantage over Trump among Hispanic voters who did not have a college degree was far narrower (55% to 41%).

One of the most pivotal groups in the 2016 election was White voters without a four-year college degree, who were critical to Trump's electoral college victory that year (nationally, he won them by a wide 36-point margin in 2016, 64% to 28%). Prior to 2016, differences in candidate preferences by education were typically much smaller than they were that year. In 2020, Trump won 65% of White non-college voters—nearly identical to his 2016 share—even as Biden outperformed Clinton among this group (33% of White non-college voters backed Biden, up from the 28% of this group Clinton won in 2016). At the same time, White voters with a college degree or higher supported Biden by roughly the same margin they had backed Clinton in 2016.

Trump's stronghold among White men without a four-year college degree loosened somewhat in 2020. While he still won this group by a little more than two-to one (66% to Biden's 31%), that 35 percentage point gap is notably smaller than the 50-point gap in the 2016 election, when 73% of White men without a college degree supported Trump, compared with 23% who supported Clinton. Meanwhile, White men with a four-year college degree have become increasingly supportive of Democratic candidates, breaking close to evenly in 2016 (47% for Clinton, 44% for Trump) but supporting Biden by a 10-point margin in 2020.

At the same time, Trump's vote share among White women without a college degree grew slightly between the 2016 and 2020 presidential elections. In 2016, White, non-college women supported Trump by a margin of 56% to 33%. By 2020, Trump's vote share rose to 64% among this group compared with 35% supporting Biden. Among white women with a college degree, support for Biden was on par with support for Clinton in 2016 (59%-40% in 2020).

Party and Ideology

Biden and Trump benefited from similar levels of party loyalty in 2020, with Trump receiving 92% support among Republicans and Republican-leaning independents and Biden getting 94% among Democrats and Democratic leaners. Comparable levels of support for each candidate were seen among Democrats (95% for Biden) and Republicans (94% for Trump), not including leaners. Among independents and those who affiliated with other parties, Biden led Trump by 52%–43%.

Ideological divisions within the parties were also apparent in the vote, with both Trump and Biden doing better among the ideological core of their parties. Trump received the votes of 97% of conservative Republicans and leaners but a smaller majority (79%) of Republicans who describe themselves as moderate or liberal. Biden took 98% of the vote among liberal Democrats and leaners and 91% among those who are moderate or conservative.

Age and Generation

A yawning age gap in voter support—a pattern that emerged in the 2004 presidential election for the first time since 1972—continues to be evident, with voters under 30 favoring Joe Biden by 24 percentage points (Biden 59%, Trump 35%).

Perhaps reflecting the enduring impact of this long-term age gap, voters ages 30 to 49 were also solidly in the Democratic candidate's camp in 2020, favoring Biden by 12 points (55%-43%), similar to Clinton's share among this age group. By contrast, older age groups divided fairly evenly between Biden and Trump, a result not too different from 2016.

These patterns also are apparent when the lens is shifted to birth cohorts, or generations—groups of voters who share birth years and perhaps formative political experiences in common, such as the popularity of the president at the time they were first eligible to vote. Voters in the youngest adult generations today—Generation Z (those ages 18 to 23 in 2020) and the Millennial generation (ages 24 to 39 in 2020)—favored Biden over Trump by a margin of 20 percentage points, though Trump gained 8 points among Millennials compared with his 2016 performance. Generation Xers, those ages 40 to 55 in 2020, divided relatively evenly (51% to 48%), as did Baby Boomers. Only among members of the Silent Generation, ages 75 to 92 in 2020, was Trump clearly favored (by 58%-42%).

Notably, Boomers and Silents (and the very small number of voters from the Greatest Generation) made up less than half of the electorate in 2020 (44%), compared with just over half in both 2016 and 2018.

Geography

The political split between America's rural areas and its suburban and urban locales remained substantial in 2020. Biden did considerably better among suburban voters in 2020 than Clinton did in 2016 (54% for Biden, 45% for Clinton). By contrast, Trump garnered the support of 65% of rural voters, including 71% of White rural voters; the latter represented an increase over the 62% he received among this group in 2016. Biden received a solid majority of votes among urban residents (66% overall), but Trump gained among urbanites relative to his performance in 2016 (33% in 2020, 24% in 2016).

Religion

Voters in 2020 sorted along religious lines in ways consistent with recent elections. Protestants constituted nearly half of all voters (46%), as they did in 2016. Within the Protestant tradition, White evangelicals accounted for 19% of all voters, but a much higher share of Trump's voters (34%). Without such broad support for Trump among White evangelicals, Biden would have beaten him by more than 20 points.

White non-evangelical Protestants voted for Trump over Biden by a 14-point margin (57%-43%), while Black Protestants were an overwhelmingly Democratic group (91% voted for Biden).

Biden, by contrast, drew strong support from religiously unaffiliated voters—atheists, agnostics, and those who say their religion is "nothing in particular." Together, these voters made up 25% of voters, which is a slightly larger share of the total electorate than White evangelicals (19%). But support for Biden among the unaffiliated was not quite as lopsided as Trump's support among White evangelicals (a 45-point margin for Biden among the unaffiliated vs. a 69-point margin for Trump among White evangelicals). Without the religiously unaffiliated, Trump would have had a 9-point popular vote margin over Biden.

White non-Hispanic Catholics were more supportive of Biden (at 42%) than they had been of Clinton in 2016 (31%), but Trump still captured a solid majority of their votes (57%). White Catholics made up 14% of all voters.

What Is Intersectionality?

Intersectionality, in social theory, is the interaction and cumulative effects of multiple forms of discrimination affecting the daily lives of individuals, particularly women of color. The term also refers more broadly to an intellectual framework for understanding how various aspects of individual identity—including race, gender, social class, and sexuality—interact to create unique experiences of privilege or oppression.

Origin and Development

The term *intersectionality* was coined by Kimberlé Crenshaw, a prominent American civil rights advocate and a leading scholar of critical race theory, in her 1989 article "Demarginalizing the Intersection of Race and Sex: A Black Feminist Critique of Antidiscrimination Doctrine, Feminist Theory, and Antiracist Politics." Crenshaw introduced the concept to address experiences of oppression that could not be adequately understood as the result of ordinary patterns of discrimination. She reiterated the concept's utility in her 1991 article "Mapping the Margins: Intersectionality, Identity Politics, and Violence Against Women of Color."

Crenshaw's work arose as a reaction to the conceptual constraints she identified in discussions among feminists and anti-racists during the 1980s. She contended that the experiences of Black women are shaped

Demographic Profiles of Trump and Biden Voters

As was the case in the 2016 and 2018 elections, the Democratic voting coalition in 2020 looked quite different from the Republican coalition in several respects. Overall, Biden voters were younger, more racially and ethnically diverse, and less likely to live in rural areas than Trump voters.

In 2020, 85% of voters who cast a ballot for Trump were White non-Hispanic; this compares with just 61% of Biden voters. These differences are roughly consistent with the share of White voters in each party's coalition in 2016.

by a combination of race- and gender-based prejudices, resulting in a distinctive convergence of discrimination and disadvantage. She also argued that such experiences could not be adequately addressed or remedied by legal and social systems that evaluate racial and sexual discrimination separately.

Well before Crenshaw, the African American sociologist W.E.B. Du Bois had theorized about how the categories of race, class, and culture mutually reinforce discrimination and social stratification, though he did not explicitly include gender in his analysis. In the 1970s the Combahee River Collective, a group of Black lesbian socialist feminists, notably addressed the "interlocking oppressions" of racism, sexism, and heteronormativity, further developing the groundwork for intersectional thinking.

The concept of intersectionality has since been broadened beyond its initial framework of race and gender. It now includes a wide spectrum of social classifications, such as socioeconomic class, sexual orientation, age, physical or intellectual disabilities, and other dimensions of individual identity. Intersectionality emphasizes that different dimensions of identity are not isolated from one another; instead, they intertwine and overlap in intricate ways, resulting in distinct advantages or disadvantages, benefits or harms.

"Intersectionality," by August Samie, Britannica.

Nearly two-in-ten voters who cast a ballot for Biden in the 2020 election (19%) were Black, identical to the share of Clinton voters in 2016 who were Black. That is significantly higher than the share of Trump voters who were Black (2%).

The community profiles of Trump and Biden voters are similar in some fundamental ways to the previous two elections – but more voters who cast ballots for Biden in 2020 say they live in a suburban area compared with Clinton's 2016 voters.

Overall, urban voters continue to constitute a larger share of the Democratic coalition compared with the Republican coalition. And rural voters remain a significantly larger portion of the Republican electorate.

However, when comparing Clinton's voters with Biden's, there are some significant shifts. In 2016, about half of Clinton's voters described their communities as suburban (48%), while 32% said they were from an urban area and 19% were from a rural area.

In 2020, suburban voters made up a majority of Biden's coalition (55%); 28% of his voters said they lived in urban areas and 17% were from rural areas.

In 2020, 31% of Trump voters had at least a four-year college degree—similar to the share of Trump voters who had a college degree in 2016. Far more Trump voters (roughly 70% in each presidential election) did not have a four-year college degree.

The Democratic electorate is more evenly divided when it comes to education. In 2020, 46% of Biden voters had at least a college degree; 53% did not have a degree.

As was the case in 2016, White voters without a four-year college degree made up a considerably larger share of GOP voters (58%) than Democratic voters (27%). At the same time, White voters with a college degree made up a larger share of Biden voters (34%) than Trump voters (27%).

In 2020, the age profiles of Democratic and Republican voters looked largely similar to 2016. Younger adults continue to make up a larger share of Democratic voters compared with

Republican voters. For example, in 2020, nearly half of Biden voters (49%) were younger than 50; that compares with 39% of Trump voters in 2020.

Protestants made up a majority of those voting Republican in 2020, just as they did in 2016. Overall, 58% of Trump voters were Protestant, compared with just 35% of Biden voters. White evangelical Protestants, in particular, remained a critical part of the Republican voting coalition, making up 34% of Trump's voters but just 6% of Biden's.

Catholics made up similar shares of Biden and Trump voters (19% and 22%, respectively); in 2016, Catholics made up a slightly higher share of Trump voters compared with Clinton voters (23% vs. 18%). Voters who were unaffiliated with any religious tradition (atheists, agnostics and those who describe themselves as "nothing in particular") made up 35% of Biden voters but just 14% of Trump voters in 2020.

Voting Methods in the 2020 Presidential Election

The 2020 election brought a huge change in how Americans cast their ballots. As some states looked to adapt to challenges in administering elections amid the COVID-19 pandemic, large numbers of voters were offered expanded access to absentee and vote-by-mail options in the 2020 election. As a result, a record number of voters said they cast their ballots this way (46%). And smaller shares of voters said they either voted in person on Election Day (27%) or in person before Election Day (27%).

A majority of absentee voters said they had previously voted this way before the 2020 election (56%). Still, a sizable share (43%) said the November election was the first time they had cast an absentee or mail ballot.

Sizable shares of voters across racial and ethnic subgroups cast absentee or mail-in ballots in the 2020 election—though there are some differences in voting methods when comparing across groups. White voters were most likely to say they voted in person on Election Day (30%). Comparably smaller shares of Black (20%) and Hispanic voters (18%) said the same.

Black voters were more likely than White or Hispanic voters to say they cast their ballot in person before Election Day (42% of Black voters, vs. 27% of Hispanic voters and 25% of White voters).

Voters ages 65 and older stand out in their voting behavior: 55% say they voted absentee or by mail in the 2020 election—13 percentage points higher than the share of adults under 65 who cast a ballot by mail.

Urban and suburban voters were considerably more likely than rural voters to say they cast their ballot by mail (50% of urban and suburban vs. 35% of rural voters). In contrast, rural voters were more likely to report voting in person on Election Day.

A majority of Biden voters said they voted absentee or by mail in the 2020 election (58%). By contrast, about a third of Trump voters (32%) voted by mail. Roughly two-thirds of Trump voters (68%) said they voted in person, either on (38%) or before (30%) Election Day. Reflecting these differences, Trump performed much better among voters who cast their ballots in person on Election Day (65% for Trump vs. 33% for Biden). These shares were reversed among absentee and mail-in voters: 65% of absentee voters said they voted for Biden, compared with 33% who voted for Trump.

Preferences were more evenly divided among those who cast their ballots in person ahead of Election Day: 52% voted for Trump while 47% voted for Biden.

Voters and Nonvoters

The 2020 general election featured the highest rate of voter turnout in more than a century, with 66% of eligible adults casting a ballot for president.

All members of the American Trends Panel who took the 2020 post-election survey—whether they voted or not – were asked which candidate they preferred in the race for president. Nonvoters—citizens for whom no record of turnout could be located or who told us they did not vote—preferred Joe Biden over Donald Trump by 15 percentage points, 50% to 35%, compared with Biden's 4-point overall advantage among voters.

Voters were nearly evenly divided on party affiliation, with 50% identifying or leaning Democratic and 48% identifying or leaning Republican, similar to the 51%-48% split in 2016. Nonvoters in 2020 were more closely divided on partisanship than they were in 2016. Among nonvoters in 2020, 46% were Democrats or leaned Democratic, while 41% were Republicans or leaned Republican. A majority of nonvoters in 2016 (55%) were Democrats or Democratic leaners compared with about four-in-ten (41%) who were Republicans or leaned toward the Republican Party.

Despite notable changes in the demographics of the two candidates' coalitions, the demographic composition of the electorate as a whole in 2020 did not differ much from that of 2016.

Although turnout was strong, stark demographic differences between voters and nonvoters similar to those seen in past U.S. elections were present in 2020, a pattern familiar to political observers.

Voters as a group were considerably older than nonvoters. Adults younger than 50 made up 45% of all voters but 68% of nonvoters—nearly identical to the pattern seen in 2016.

But generational change in the electorate was quite apparent. Very few members of Gen Z (born 1997 and later) were eligible to vote in the 2016 electorate, and they made up just 1% of all voters that year. In 2020, they were 8% of the total, though their lower rate of turnout compared with older age cohorts is reflected in the fact that they were 15% of eligible nonvoters. At the other end of the generational spectrum, members of the Silent and Greatest generations (born 1945 and earlier) fell from 16% of all voters in 2016 to just 8% in 2020, but their turnout rates remained among the highest of all generations.

Turnout differences by race and ethnicity persisted as well. White non-Hispanic adults were 72% of voters in 2020 but just 55% of nonvoting citizens. Black Americans made up 11% of voters, but a slightly larger share (14%) of nonvoting citizens, and Hispanic adults were 10% of voters but 20% of nonvoting citizens. Asian Americans (a relatively small but fast-growing group in the U.S.) made up 4% of voters and an identical share of nonvoting citizens (note: nonvoters in this analysis do not include noncitizens).

Some of the largest differences between voters and nonvoters are seen on education and income. College graduates made up 39% of all voters in 2020 (about the same as in 2016) but only 17% of nonvoters. Adults with a high school education or less were 29% of all voters but half of nonvoters.

Periodical and Internet Sources Bibliography

The following articles have been selected to supplement the diverse views presented in this chapter.

Simon Bein, "What Identity Does Democracy Need? The Necessity and Danger of Political Polarization," The Loop, https://theloop.ecpr.eu/what-identity-does-democracy-need-the-necessity-and-danger-of-political-polarisation/.

Lee H. Hamilton, "Are We Doomed to Polarization in Government?," *The Epoch Times*, November 26, 2015. https://www.theepochtimes.com/article/are-we-doomed-to-polarization-in-government-795590.

Aoife Paul Healy, "Identity Politics Aren't Going Anywhere but Political Polarization Might," *Mount Holyoke News*, April 15, 2024. http://www.mountholyokenews.com/opinion/2024/4/8/do-not-publish-identity-politics-arent-going-anywhere-but-polarization-could.

Ezra Klein, "Toward a Better Theory of Identity Politics," Vox, January 23, 2020. https://www.vox.com/podcasts/2020/1/23/21077236/ezra-klein-show-book-why-were-polarized-identity-politics.

Matthew S. Levendusky, "Americans, Not Partisans: Can Priming American National Identity Reduce Affective Polarization?," *The Journal of Politics*, January 2018. https://www.journals.uchicago.edu/doi/abs/10.1086/693987.

Jennifer McCoy and Benjamin Press, "What Happens When Democracies Become Perniciously Polarized?," Carnegie Endowment for International Peace, January 18, 2022. https://carnegieendowment.org/research/2022/01/what-happens-when-democracies-become-perniciously-polarized?lang=en.

Verena Schoenmueller, Oded Netzer, and Florian Stahl, "Frontiers: Polarized America: Political Polarization to Preference Polarization," *Marketing Science*, December 8, 2022. https://pubsonline.informs.org/doi/full/10.1287/mksc.2022.1408.

Ryan Strickler, "Deliberate with the Enemy? Polarization, Social Identity, and Attitudes Toward Disagreement," *Political Research Quarterly*, March 2018. https://www.jstor.org/stable/26600446.

Elizabeth Whitworth, "Are Identity Politics in America to Blame for Growing Polarization?" Shortform, June 26, 2023. https://www.shortform.com/blog/identity-politics-in-america/.

For Further Discussion

Chapter 1

1. What are some examples of how identity played a role in politics in American history?
2. How are wokeism and cancel culture related to identity politics?
3. Based on what you've read in the viewpoints in this chapter, have the definition or public perception of identity politics changed over time?

Chapter 2

1. How does social media impact identity politics?
2. In what ways do media outlets characterize social media and political polarization? How does this impact identity politics and political polarization?
3. Based on what you've read in this chapter, what type of media has the greatest impact on polarizing social identity groups? Use evidence from this chapter to support your answer.

Chapter 3

1. In what way has identity politics helped marginalized people?
2. Based on what you've read in this chapter, do you think identity politics have gone too far? Why or why not?
3. How would you define wokeism, based on viewpoints in this chapter and throughout the book?

Chapter 4

1. The viewpoint in this chapter by Hannah Hartig, Andrew Daniller, Scott Keeter, and Ted Van Green notes that voter turnout has increased as political polarization and appeals to identity politics have also increased. Do you think increased

voter turnout is a positive effect in this situation? Why or why not?

2. Based on what you've read in the viewpoint by Arash Javanbakht, what role does tribalism have in identity politics and politics in general? Do you think identity politics are possible without tribalism? Explain your answer.
3. Using evidence from this chapter and beyond, why do various types of social identity—including those based on race, gender, geography, sexuality, and education—allow people to predict how someone will vote? Has this always been the case?

Organizations to Contact

The editors have compiled the following list of organizations concerned with the issues debated in this book. The descriptions are derived from materials provided by the organizations. All have publications or information available for interested readers. The list was compiled on the date of publication of the present volume; the information provided here may change. Be aware that many organizations take several weeks or longer to respond to inquiries, so allow as much time as possible.

American Civil Liberties Union (ACLU)

125 Broad Street, 18th floor
New York, NY 10004
(212) 549-2500
email: aclupreferences@aclu.org
website: www.aclu.org

The American Civil Liberties Union uses its resources to fight for and preserve individual rights and freedoms in the United States. Some of the key rights they are currently fighting to protect include abortion care, trans rights, and voting rights.

Campus Pride

PO Box 240473
Charlotte, NC 28224
(704) 277-6710
email: info@campuspride.org
website: www.campuspride.org

Campus Pride is the only national non-profit organization for student leaders and campus groups working to foster a safer college environment for LGBTQ+ students. It offers leadership training, support programs, and services to help support this goal.

Center for American Progress

133 H Street Northwest
Washington, DC 20005
(202) 682-1611
website: www.americanprogress.org

The Center for American Progress is a liberal public policy research and advocacy organization focused on economic and social issues. It seeks to move the country forward in a progressive direction.

Democracy Matters

201 Riverview Drive
Poughkeepsie, NY 12601
(315) 725-4211
website: www.democracymatters.org

Democracy Matters helps students organize projects connecting pro-democracy reforms on such issues as the environment, civil rights, education, and health care. Its goal is to reduce the role of money and increase the role of activists in the American political system.

National LGBTQ Task Force

1050 Connecticut Ave. NW, Suite 65500
Washington, DC 20035
(202) 393-5177
website: thetaskforce.org

This organization seeks to achieve freedom and justice for lesbian, gay, bisexual, transgender, queer people, and their families through proactive, targeted, and change-inducing initiatives. It works to ensure the LGBTQ+ community has a voice in policy, legislation, and society.

Project Mobilize

7674 W. 63rd Street
Summit, IL 60501
website: www.mobilize.org

Project Mobilize is a network of leaders targeting young people that seeks to create positive change within the political system and through existing organizations. It also works to invest in new ideas that would help unify Americans in a progressive manner.

Race Forward

PO Box 96353
Washington, DC 20090
email: development@raceforward.org
website: www.raceforward.org

Race Forward works with communities to build the collective power necessary to counter structural racism. It connects with people and organizations to create and inspire positive change in a multiracial society.

Transgender Law Center

PO Box 70976
Oakland, CA 94612
email: into@transgenderlawcenter.org
website: https://transgenderlawcenter.org

This group is the largest national trans-led organization advocating self-determination for all people. It organizes, assists, informs and empowers individual community members towards a long-term, national, trans-led movement for liberation.

Young America's Foundation

11480 Commerce Park Drive, Suite 600
Reston, VA 20191
(703) 318-9608
website: www.yaf.org

This conservative student group seeks to increase the number of students that are motivated toward ideas of individual freedom, a strong national defense, free enterprise, and traditional values. It offers conferences, educational materials, seminars, and internships to support this goal.

Young Democratic Socialists of America

705 Maiden Lane, Suite 702
New York, NY, 10038
(917) 830-8416
website: www.mobilize.org

This political organization works to build the power of students, campus communities, and youth to fight for equality, justice, and democratic socialism. It aims to produce a more unified, inclusive, and forward-thinking nation.

Bibliography of Books

Khalilah L. Brown-Dean. *Identity Politics in the United States*. Queensland, Australia: Polity Books, 2019.

Frank Bruni. *The Age of Grievance*. New York, NY: Avid Reader Press, 2024.

Norman Finkelstein. *I'll Burn That Bridge When I Get to It! Heretical Thought on Identity Politics, Cancel Culture, and Academic Freedom*. New York, NY: Sublation Media, 2023.

Francis Fukuyama. *Identity: Contemporary Identity Politics and the Struggle for Recognition*. London, UK: Profile Books: 2018.

Richard Hanania. *The Origins of Woke: Civil Rights Law, Corporate America and the Triumph of Identity Politics*. Northampton, MA: Broadside Books, 2023.

Victor Davis Hanson. *The Dying Citizen: How Progressive Elites, Tribalism and Globalization are Destroying the Idea of America*. New York, NY: Basic Books, 2021.

Robert Kagan. *Rebellion: How Antiliberalism Is Tearing America Apart — Again*. New York, NY: Knopf, 2024.

Mark Lilla. *The Once and Future Liberal: After Identity Politics*. New York, NY: Harper, 2024.

Natalie Masouka and Jane Junn. *The Politics of Belonging: Race, Public Opinion and Immigration*. Chicago, IL: University of Chicago Press, 2013.

Joshua Mitchell. *American Awakening: Identity Politics and Other Afflictions of Our Time*. New York, NY: Encounter Books, 2020.

Vivek Ramaswamy. *Nation of Victims: Identity Politics, the Death of Merit, and the Path Back to Excellence*. New York, NY: Center Street Publishing, 2022.

Olivier Roy, Cynthia Schoch, and Trista Selous. *The Crisis of Culture: Identity Politics and the Empire of Norms*. New York, NY: Oxford University Press, 2024.

Todd Shaw, Louis DiSipio, Dianne Pinderhughes, and Toni-Michelle C. Travis. *Uneven Roads: An Introduction to U.S. Racial and Ethnic Politics*. Washington, DC: CQ Press, 2018.

Olufemi O. Taiwo. *Elite Capture: How the Powerful Took Over Identity Politics (And Everything Else)*. Chicago, IL: Haymarket Books, 2022.

Fareed Zakaria. *Age of Revolutions: Progress and Backlash from 1600 to the Present*. New York, NY: W.W. Norton & Co., 2024.

Index

D

E

F

G

T

V

W

X

Y